A Synthesis of Qualitative Studies of Writing Center Tutoring, 1983–2006

This book is part of the Peter Lang Education list.
Every volume is peer reviewed and meets
the highest quality standards for content and production.

PETER LANG
New York • Washington, D.C./Baltimore • Bern
Frankfurt • Berlin • Brussels • Vienna • Oxford

REBECCA DAY BABCOCK, KELLYE MANNING, TRAVIS ROGERS,
WITH COURTNEY GOFF AND AMANDA MCCAIN

A SYNTHESIS OF QUALITATIVE STUDIES OF WRITING CENTER TUTORING, 1983–2006

PETER LANG
New York • Washington, D.C./Baltimore • Bern
Frankfurt • Berlin • Brussels • Vienna • Oxford

Library of Congress Cataloging-in-Publication Data

Babcock, Rebecca Day.
A synthesis of qualitative studies of writing center tutoring,
1983–2006 / Rebecca Day Babcock, Kellye Manning,
Travis Rogers, Courtney Goff, Amanda McCain.
pages cm
Includes bibliographical references and index.
1. Writing centers. 2. English language—Rhetoric—Study and teaching
(Higher)—Evaluation. 3. Report writing—Study and teaching (Higher)—
Evaluation. 4. Tutors and tutoring. I. Manning, Kellye. II. Rogers, Travis.
III. Goff, Courtney. IV. McCain, Amanda. V. Title.
PE1404.B2235 808'.042071173—dc23 2012011447
ISBN 978-1-4331-1786-2 (hardcover)
ISBN 978-1-4331-1787-9 (paperback)
ISBN 978-1-4539-0857-0 (e-book)

Bibliographic information published by **Die Deutsche Nationalbibliothek**.
Die Deutsche Nationalbibliothek lists this publication in the "Deutsche Nationalbibliografie"; detailed bibliographic data is available on the Internet at http://dnb.d-nb.de/.

The paper in this book meets the guidelines for permanence and durability of the Committee on Production Guidelines for Book Longevity of the Council of Library Resources.

29 Broadway, 18th floor, New York, NY 10006
www.peterlang.com

Printed in the United States of America

TABLE OF CONTENTS

FOREWORD

It is a pleasure to write the foreword for this synthesis of qualitative studies of writing center tutoring. In the field of writing center studies, empirical data has only recently begun to qualify as evidence for theory-practice. Since research syntheses require that the studies surveyed conform to the RAD (replicable, aggregable, data-driven) rubric (Haswell, 2005), comparability is actually possible. And while quantitative methodologies have their place in writing center research, it is qualitative methodologies, requiring "thick description," which I believe best capture the rich detail of writing center theory-practice.

Babcock, Manning, Rogers and colleagues have taken on a project no one else in the field, to my knowledge, has attempted. Certainly, there are writing center scholars who have compiled excellent annotated bibliographies, including those of writing center scholarship (DeShaw, Mullin, & DeCiccio, 2000); writing center theses and dissertations (Lerner, 2010a); writing center assessment articles (Lerner & Kail, 2009); writing center history (Lerner, 2010b); and professional resources (IWCA, 2009). Babcock herself has been a Modern Language Association bibliographer for seven years. Writing a synthesis, however, is an entirely different proposition: it requires summary, analysis, comparison and contrast, and evaluation of sources. In fields outside of writing center studies, including medicine, education, and applied linguistics, research syntheses (sometimes termed state-of-the-art articles or review articles) save scholars valuable time and energy in their search to stake out research "territory."

From the beginning, writing center work has been cast as highly collaborative (Bruffee, 1995; Harris, 1992). And collaborative this book certainly is. After studying nine sources on grounded theory (several of them co-authored), eight readers—expert, semi-expert, and naïve—analyzed fifty-five documents reporting qualitative research studies. The readers received feedback on their first draft from eleven of the study authors. One might argue, then, that the text before you represents the collaboration of twenty-eight or more individuals. This, too, is common in research syntheses, and the diversity of input clearly increases the perceived validity and reliability of the product.

Readers of this work will come away with trustworthy, data-driven information about personal characteristics of tutors and tutees; external influences on writing tutorials; communication features of tutorials; tutor and tutee roles; emotional factors in tutorials; and session outcomes. Each content-focused chapter concludes with brief summary of themes emerging from the data, providing memorable "takeaways" for the reader. The book's conclusion functions as a synthesis of syntheses related to tutorial outcomes and a call for future research.

As a writing center director, I was curious about how I might use this book in staff and tutor training. I asked a question that commonly comes up in our discussions: "How can we avoid the tutor-centered consultation?" The research studies synthesized on pages 12–24 of this book offered these responses: Writing tutors should be "careful" about their role as authorities (Bell, 1989b) and avoid imposing "ideal texts" on student writing (Roswell, 1992). They should strive to engage the tutee in talk (Stachera, 2003), especially if they are older than the tutee (Wolcott, 1989), have worked with the same tutee before (Lerner, 1996), or are tackling grammar issues in the writer's text (Vallejo, 2004). This is valuable information for my staff. And if any writing center scholar decides to research this topic, he or she has read an incipient review of the literature and become aware of methodologies useful in collecting data for a replication or brand-new study.

A Synthesis of Qualitative Studies of Writing Tutoring excludes quantitative, anecdotal, and lore-based studies as well as any research done outside of college and university writing centers. To some readers, that may be disappointing, but to me, it is one of the strengths of the book. Narrowing the methodological scope of synthesis allows the authors to go deeper, creating a nuanced picture of current research in academic writing centers.

Terese Thonus
University of Kansas

References

Bruffee, K. A. (1995). Peer tutoring and the "conversation of mankind." In Murphy, C., & J. Law (Eds.), *Landmark Essays on Writing Centers* (pp. 87–98). Davis, CA: Hermagoras Press.

DeShaw, D., Mullin, J., & DeCiccio, A. (2000). Twenty years of *Writing Center Journal* scholarship: An annotated bibliography. *Writing Center Journal, 20* (2), 39–72.

Harris, M. (1992). Collaboration is not collaboration is not collaboration: Writing center tutorials vs. peer-response groups. *College Composition & Communication, 43*(3), 369–383.

International Writing Centers Association. (2009). *Bibliography of resources for writing center professionals.* Retrieved from http://writingcenters.org/wp-content/uploads/2010/12/bibliography_of_resources.pdf

Lerner, N. (2010a). *Dissertations and theses on writing centers.* Retrieved from http://writingcenters.org/wp-content/uploads/2010/12/WC_Dissertations_and_Theses_RevJuly2010.pdf

Lerner, N. (2010b). Chronology of published descriptions of writing laboratories/clinics, 1894–1977. *WPA-CompPile Research Bibliographies,* No. 9. Retrieved from http://comppile.org/wpa/bibliographies/Bib9/Lerner.pdf

Lerner, N., & Kail, H. (2004). *Writing center assessment bibliography.* Retrieved from http://web.mit.edu/nlerner/Public/WCAssessmentBib.pdf

ACKNOWLEDGMENTS

This book would not have been possible without the support and encouragement of our family and friends, especially Mike Babcock. Special thanks goes to Nick Sutcliffe of Leeds Metropolitan University for research methodology assistance. Thanks also to Marshalla Hutson, Sherry McKibben, Neal Lerner, Jane Sell, and Gavin Fairbairn for research assistance and advice, and to Lee D. Day for preparing the index. Thanks to the outstanding staff of the University Writing Center of the University of Texas of the Permian Basin, past and present. This research was supported by the UTPB Fund for Academic Excellence and a UTPB start-up grant.

CHAPTER ONE

Introduction

This book attempts to synthesize the qualitative research on writing centers that appeared in a 20-year span toward the end of the 20th century. The original idea for this synthesis came when the principal investigator, Rebecca Day Babcock, prepared questions for her doctoral comprehensive exam in writing centers. One of the questions was, "Is there a writing center theory, and if so, what is it?" She found that there was no one common writing center theory, but rather a set of practices and a pattern of taking theories from other disciplines and applying them to writing centers. Shamoon and Burns, in their "A Critique of Pure Tutoring" noted that writing center practice is "less the product of research or examined practice" and "more like articles of faith" (1995, p. 135). Babcock realized that in order to find out what a unified theory of writing center tutoring would look like, it would be necessary to look at actual studies of tutoring and see what theories emerged.

Background of Writing Centers

The precursor to today's writing centers was the laboratory approach, which began in the late 19th century, about 20 years after the institution of the college writing course (Lerner, 2006; 2009). In these methods, students composed while trained instructors supervised and intervened in their composing processes as necessary. These methods continued into the 1930s at the University of Minnesota General College. Many early 20th century published accounts were of high school contexts, and these early approaches resembled the workshop approach currently advocated by Nancie Atwell. The Dalton Plan, devised in 1922 by Helen Parkhurst, consisted of individual work and conferences in all subjects (Lerner, 2009). Closer to our contemporary views of writing centers were programs started in the 1930s at the University of Minnesota and at the University of Iowa where one-on-one and small group tutoring were practiced (Carino, 1995). In

1950, Moore listed "individual tutoring" (p. 388) as something apart from the writing laboratory or clinic. Clearly, early labs and clinics took many different forms, and like today, there was no consensus of what they should be. Nevertheless, they were a strong presence in American colleges until seemingly falling away from popularity sometime in the 1950s. For instance, there was a workshop session on writing laboratories at almost every CCCC from 1950–1956, but Lerner's (2010) bibliography showed a trickling off of citations after 1958, with an upsurge after 1965.

With the coming of open admissions, writing centers and labs began to reappear and this history is well known and documented. In 1984(a) North justified the program and curriculum of peer tutoring, as did Bruffee (1984). In that same year, Bloom (1984) proved once and for all that tutoring is the most effective strategy to improve students' performance. Even though North called for research in 1984(b), little actual research on the effectiveness of specific tutoring practices has been conducted (Jones, 2001). Research has continued to be rather sparse over the years, and calls to research have continued to appear. Rogers (2008) noted that "Most writing center claims of success are not evidence-based" (p. 33), and that "the word *successful* is often used interchangeably with the word *effective* in current literature on tutoring" (p.115, italics original).

Writing Center Research

The first call to writing center research appeared in E. F. Linquist's dissertation (1927; qtd in Lerner, 2006, p. 5): "one of the most important functions of the laboratory supervisor [is] to engage in…research and study that will effect…improvements." Although Linquist called for research on methods, actual early research on writing centers was in the form of surveys more geared to administration and institutional issues rather than teaching methods. Some of these were Thornton's 1938 thesis "A Limited Survey of the Laboratory Method in Teaching English Composition," Moore's 1950 article in *College English,* "The Writing Clinic and the Writing Laboratory," and Shouse's 1953 dissertation "The Writing Laboratory in Colleges and Universities" (all qtd in Lerner, 2006). Although several early research studies were conducted (i.e. Ferster, 1937; Horner, 1929), little more was done (or at least published) until the 1980s. Horner (1929) did an experiment. He studied two groups of high school students, one taught by the laboratory method and one taught by the recitation method. It is interesting to note that peer review was part of the recitation method as well as lectures and demonstrations about writing and discussions over readings, and all writing was completed at home and time spent working was logged. In the laboratory method all composing was done in the classroom and the teacher would go around and conference with the students. Horner found a very small gain in writing skills among the laboratory group, but the significant finding was that they spent half the time working to achieve the same results. The laboratory method was more efficient. Ferster's work was not a formal research study but rather an informal implementation of a three-day experience of a writing lab for college freshmen. She concluded that the laboratory approach would be profitable for all subjects rather than just English.

Some examples of second-wave quantitative studies are Stay (1983), who studied revision in the tutoring session and David & Bubolz (1985), who studied improvements in writing skills of students who were tutored in the writing center. Pre- and post-test scores were compared. There was no control group. The only recent example of an experiment that we have found is Cumming & So (1996). Most writing center studies to date have been qualitative, and the earliest one considered in this study came a year before North's call to research (Frank, 1983). Qualitative studies often use data such as observation, interview, and collection of relevant documents.

Current State of Writing Centers

For readers unfamiliar with writing centers, it might be prudent to explain some of the current and enduring issues. Student-centeredness and collaboration have been buzzwords in writing center studies for some time now. It is writing center dogma or formalism that that tutors should adopt a student-centered or collaborative approach to tutorials, and very little research or, indeed, questioning of such a stance has occurred (See Shamoon and Burns, 1995, for the now-classic definition and critique of this phenomenon).

The idea of student-centeredness began with the realization of late 20th century writing center and writing lab directors that there was unease, even distrust of the work of writing tutors on the part of English department faculties and others. The work was often misperceived as a sort of dishonest academic exercise wherein an accomplished writer (the tutor) transformed the inferior work of a less accomplished writer (the tutee) to achieve better grades. A student-centered practice then came to mean that the tutor would take a hands-off or minimalist approach to the tutorial. All ideas, all work, all editorial marks would be generated by the writer; the tutor was a guide or facilitator, but anything more smacked of academic dishonesty (Clark & Healy, 1996). For instance, tutors have typically been trained to elicit rather than provide information to tutees. Thus, tutors found themselves in the awkward position of asking questions such as, "Why do you have a comma here?" of a writer with very poor punctuation skills, knowing full well the writer could not answer the question.

These issues of collaboration, student centeredness, directive vs. non-directive tutoring and the place of grammar have been at the forefront for decades. Although some may think these controversies are dead, they are not (Corbett, 2008). Most of these issues, however, have been theorized and anecdotalized but not actually researched. Thompson Whyte, Shannon, Muse, Miller, Chappell et al (2009) have done a lot to redress this oversight. Babcock & Thonus (2012) have produced a book advocating writing center practice based on research rather than theory or anecdote. The idea for that book actually grew out of this project. The point of the present study, however, was not to investigate these issues, but to come to the data with no pre-judgments of what we would find. Therefore we were not looking specifically for any of these issues.

As we explained above, writing center studies lacks an overarching common theory. Some may ask why we need theory. As one reviewer asked, "What does theory mean for the context of the writing center community? What is its value? Why should we seek to theorize what happens?" Without a theory each tutoring session would be a fresh encounter, building on nothing that came before. It would begin from nothing and have to be re-invented each time. This project grew out of the belief of a need for a grounded theory, a theory grounded in data rather than in abstractions in order to present a complete model of what actually happens in tutoring sessions. Rather than borrow theory from other disciplines, we need to construct our own. Fallon (2010) called for scholarship that represents the actual experiences of tutors. All the studies in this synthesis contained actual data from tutoring sessions, the voices of tutors and tutees. Fallon also pinpointed the importance of relationships. As Fallon suggested, this study attempts to reverse the flow of theory from abstractions down to practice, to a ground-up approach through looking at actual data from tutors and tutees and abstracting theoretical models from them.

The present study aims at providing a look at what actually happens in writing center tutorials—how participants react to various approaches—and we provide a theoretical framework in the conclusion to help formulate how theory and practice can produce increasingly effective tutorials. We further open our findings to every interested reader to further the conversation and research as we seek to understand more clearly just exactly what happens in tutoring sessions.

Background of the Study

Because there has been so little literature on metaresearch in writing center studies, this project focuses on the description of what goes on in a tutoring session and seeks to build a theory from that foundation. We contend that writing center tutoring, rather than being based on research, has been based on common practice, lore, and theory imposed from outside disciplines such as psychology and literary studies. The writing center community is ready for a book such as this that synthesizes the research to date, especially since so much of it is buried away in dissertation studies.

Babcock completed a grounded theory study based on naturalistic data for her dissertation (Babcock, 2005). In preparation for this work, Babcock read the *Basics of Qualitative Research* by Strauss and Corbin (1990) and saw that grounded theory would be a good approach to use in a synthesis of qualitative studies of writing center tutoring. In correspondence with colleagues about the project, she learned that the idea was valuable but that the task was too big for one or even two people to undertake: The sheer amount of work and need for triangulation of ideas necessitated a team approach. Strauss & Corbin also mentioned a research team approach in their book and Babcock thought that would be an ideal way to conduct the study. The problem at that point was finding collaborators. When Babcock was hired at the University of Texas Permian Basin she was asked to provide a research agenda. Since she had been thinking of a synthesis (which she had originally called a meta-analysis until she learned the difference, which is that meta-analyses are done with quantitative studies, and there are not enough quantitative studies of writing centers to do such a study), she listed the synthesis as one of her potential research projects and was provided with a start-up grant to complete it. Babcock had been in contact with Kellye Manning of the UTPB Writing Center and proposed the project to her. Manning enthusiastically agreed to participate. You hold the result of this collaboration in your hands: A grounded theory analysis of qualitative research studies of writing centers, the first volume of its kind.

Methods

Babcock and Manning assembled a research team who read and analyzed studies using a grounded theory approach with qualitative studies as the data source. The research team consisted of three sets of readers: experts, semi-experts, and non-experts or naïve readers. We thought it important to include these three levels of readers in order to get different perspectives on the studies. The inclusion of naïve readers is supported by a reviewer of the article "Grounded Theory Methodology: An Overview" by Strauss and Corbin in the *Handbook of Qualitative Research*: "Naïve researchers 'may be even more likely to see things that don't make sense, and therefore ask questions why? Or may be more likely to ask why don't you think about it (do it) this way?'" Strauss and Corbin commented, "[The reviewer] has a point, given that new perspectives can precipitate significant and even radical issues" (1994, p. 284). The inclusion of these naïve readers allowed us a look from a different perspective, as they noticed things that we would not.

Recruiting team members. Manning was enthusiastic and asked the writing center tutors to join the project. Three tutors agreed to participate. Amanda McCain was Babcock's graduate assistant at the time, so she joined the team as part of her research duties. The start-up grant allowed Babcock to hire student research assistants, so she advertised generally for student assistants among the undergraduate population. She received many applications and vetted them carefully. She hired Courtney Goheen (now Goff) and Valerie Chavez—both were freshmen—and Chavez was also in Babcock's writing class. Babcock and Manning served as the experts on the team. The three undergraduate writing tutors and one graduate student—Jade Cothran, Travis Rogers, Loy Pearce, and Amanda McCain—served as the semi-experts. The non-experts—naïve readers—were Valerie Chavez and Courtney Goheen (now Goff).

Preparing the team. To prepare the research team for the investigation we did a series of readings. We began with background readings which Babcock distributed in paper copies and online. She also was able to purchase copies of *Basics of Qualitative Research* so each reader or pair (some worked closely together) would have their own copy for reference. The readings were as follows:

- *Basics of Qualitative Research* (2nd ed; Strauss & Corbin, 1998)
- "Doing Qualitative Analysis" (Highlen & Finley, 1996)
- "Ecological Triangulation: An Approach for Qualitative Meta-Synthesis" (Banning, n.d.)
- "Grounded Theory: A Thumbnail Sketch" (Dick, n.d.)
- "Grounded Theory Methodology: An Overview" (Strauss & Corbin, 1994)
- "Meta-Synthesis of Qualitative Studies: From Theory to Practice" (Reis et al., 2002)
- "The Process of Synthesizing Qualitative Research: A Case Study" (Suri, 1999)
- Selections from "Research Synthesis and Meta-Analysis" (Cooper & Lindsay, 1998)

- "What Are We Talking About?: A Content Analysis of the *Writing Lab Newsletter*, April 1985 to October 1998" (Bell, 1989a)

Bibliographic methods and inclusion/exclusion criteria. Babcock based the initial bibliography on studies she had collected for her comprehensive exams and dissertation research. To this she added sources provided by Neal Lerner. Then, the research team took over. Members of the team looked at online archives of *The Writing Lab Newsletter* and *The Writing Center Journal,* browsed library stacks, and searched online databases. We added these sources to the bibliography, resulting in a final data set of twenty-six dissertations, three book chapters, twenty-eight journal articles, and one paper from a conference proceeding for a total of fifty-eight sources included in the synthesis. Unfortunately, the team was unable to find any single-authored books of qualitative studies of individual writing center tutoring. The period covered is 1983–2006.

The initial inclusion criteria were qualitative studies of writing center tutoring. An exception was made for studies that used both qualitative and quantitative methods. The studies also had to make use of primary data, such as observation of tutoring sessions and interviews with participants. Our grounded theory project had the study data as our data, rather than the researchers' conclusions. For that reason we excluded any studies that did not directly report their data. The cutoff for case studies was that they needed to be clearly stated as case studies with a clear methodology and research questions. Anecdotes or narratives about tutoring were ruled out. Furthermore, since the population we are interested in is college students, any articles about high school or elementary school writing centers were eliminated. However, we decided to include articles about graduate student writers. After compiling the initial bibliography, we reserved the right to eliminate articles which, on further reading, proved to be inappropriate. We also devised a matrix to look at questionable articles more objectively (see Appendix A). Upon double-checking sources when writing the draft, any articles that were subsequently found to be inappropriate were cut from the study and not used in the analysis. For instance, several well-known studies were excluded because they were quantitative or because upon reflection they proved to be other than data-driven studies about actual tutoring in a writing center.

Grounded theory work. Once the bibliography was prepared, Babcock began accumulating articles and ordering dissertations through interlibrary loan and ProQuest and distributing them to the readers. The research team met weekly to debrief and discuss the findings and concepts as they were generated. In the beginning, several readers read the same article so we could make sure we were accurate in the coding. At least two readers read each study and a third reader read any study that was extremely difficult to code and analyze. As the study progressed, one reader read each study and a second or third reader took on any particularly difficult studies or reviewed those that needed to be judged for appropriateness. For each article or dissertation read, readers prepared any number of coding memos and posted these to an online repository and also made copies to distribute at meetings. Coding memos were summaries and analyses of the categorical terms that emerged from the data, such as "knowledge" or key terms like "authority". Thus, when we read an article we noted any concept that emerged from the data and recorded it and the supporting study data in a coding memo. The codes were developed in a list and were constantly updated. We negotiated these codes as we went along, especially when we saw similar phenomena that could be combined under one code, or items that had similar sounding names but actually were different things. For instance, we began to see that "authority" and "authoritarian" were two different codes and concepts that ended up in two separate categories. Some articles produced several coding memos, as one memo was written for each code. Axial coding came later as we tried to make connections between the codes and form them into categories. Emerging relationships between codes and categories were mapped out graphically (see figure 1; Visio chart). We not only created the Visio chart, which evolved and changed as our understandings evolved (the organization of the final document continued to evolve after we completed work on the chart), but we physically stacked note cards on a table, moving them about until we could categorize and make sense of the details we had recorded. For instance, *roles* was originally tied to *communication* under a larger category of *rapport*, until we realized that *rapport* was actually an *outcome*, and *emotion* and *temperament* were connected until we realized they belonged to separate categories.

As the research progressed, the team wrote analytic, theoretical and operational memos (Strauss & Corbin, 1990). Analytic memos advanced our understanding of what we were seeing. Theoretical memos began to tentatively articulate a theory of what we were seeing. Operational memos were suggestions or directions for the actual operation of the team. Rogers recalled that being in an environment where he was tutoring and reading about tutoring on a nearly daily basis, he became more conscious of his behavior during tutoring sessions and began to observe his clients' behavior and his own. These small insights contributed to the clarification of the coding and organization on several occasions. This is the advantage of the semi-expert reader who can bring practical experience to the task.

The research team focused on the actual data presented in the studies rather than commentary or conclusions by the authors, and were careful to include in the memos and analysis only the material from the study data, not the researchers' conclusions. Several times we came to different conclusions about what was going on in the data than the source authors did. Outside theories only came into play only after our grounded theory work was complete. Manning had been reading Vygotsky, and his work came up several times in discussions as we tried to make sense of what we were seeing. We also read some scholars whose work was based on Vygotsky's that allowed us to connect our findings to theoretical concepts (ie Donato, 1994, Aljaafreh & Lantolf, 1994).The remaining team members (some of the undergraduates dropped out) drafted the resulting study and presented their results at the 2007 IWCA conference in Houston (Babcock, Manning, McCain, & Rogers, 2007). Our understandings continued to grow and change as we wrote and revised the document over the next several years.

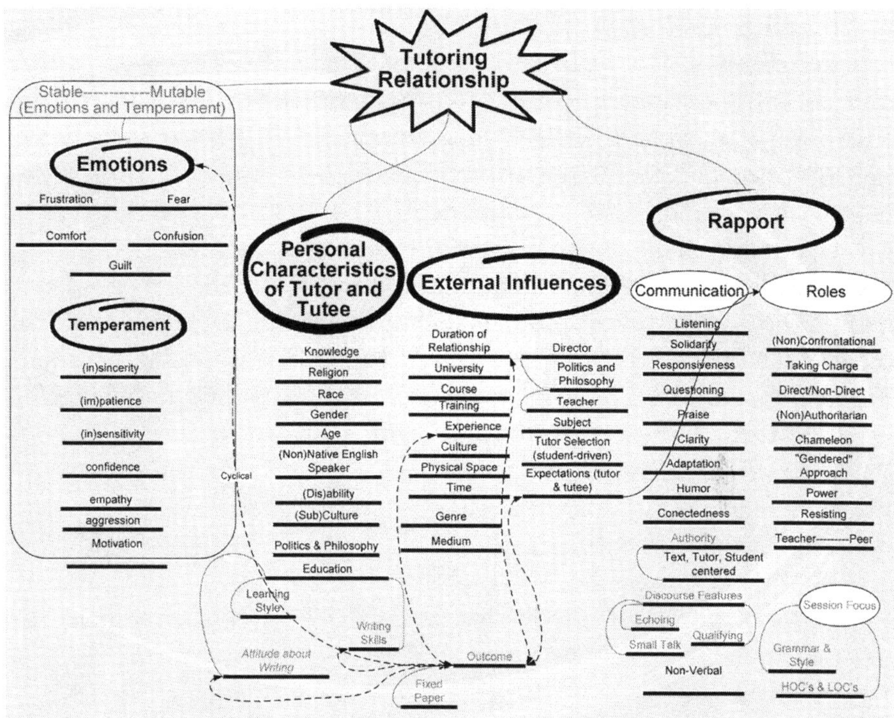

Figure 1. Visio chart used to brainstorm flow of tutoring. (Figure made by Valerie "Jade" Cothran and updated by Daniel Price)

Member checking. Once the draft was completed to our satisfaction, all living authors of studies included in the analysis were emailed and asked if they would be willing to participate in member-checking activities. Those who responded positively were sent a copy of a draft for feedback—either the entire study or just those portions of the study that mentioned their work—their responses were taken into account in subsequent revisions. About half of the source authors chose to participate in the member-checking (twenty agreed to participate and eleven followed through with responses). The use of member-checking allowed us to verify that we had interpreted the studies correctly.

Results/Findings. Through our grounded theory analysis we developed a theory or framework for writing center tutoring. We concluded that this process can be said to have occurred during any tutorial session: Tutor and tutee encounter each other and bring background, expectations, and personal characteristics into a context composed of outside influences. Through the use of roles and communication they interact, creating the session focus, the energy of which is generated through a continuum of collaboration and conflict. The temperament and emotions of the tutor and tutee interplay with the other factors in the session. The confluence of these factors results in the outcome of the session (affective, cognitive, and material). Wolcott (1989) put it well when she wrote that "each conference represents a unique blending of variables—tutor personality, tutor priorities, student personality, student background, and student text" (p. 25). The following is a detailed breakdown of what the research studies we analyzed said about the parts of this process.

CHAPTER TWO

Personal Characteristics

According to our grounded theory analysis, the personal characteristics of the tutor and tutee contribute to the creation of the tutoring session and the participants' relationships. These characteristics have to do with the participants' backgrounds and identities that they bring with them to the session. Severino (1992) found that these characteristics of "interactional style...personality and pedagogy...set the stage and determine the structure and balance of the...session" (p. 59). Some tutors in our data made undue assumptions about the personal characteristics of their tutees because they failed to ask them pertinent questions about their background and status. Our data showed us that sometimes personal characteristics and temperament combine and result in chemistry, which, although undefined, is an important factor in the connectedness participants feel in the tutoring session. Eckard (2001) quoted a participant discussing "chemistry" as "what makes students come back to the Center. Without a connection, they just drift away" (p. 125). McGuire (1969) discussed three main influences in attitude change: The credibility, attractiveness, and power of the interlocutor. Most of the following material could be associated with any of these three valences. For instance, the tutor's age, older vs. younger, could be seen as contributing to credibility, attractiveness, and power.

Knowledge

Both tutors and tutees have a range of and relation to knowledge of the topic at hand and of writing processes and practices. Roswell (1992) found that "students who identified strongly with a particular discourse community (the discourse of biology or of literary theory) sought out tutors with similar orientations" (p. 181). Jordan (2003) found that tutors thought their knowledge gave them power and authority as a tutor. Sometimes knowledge or lack of it influenced the tutoring practices in the session. Kiedaisch and Dinitz (1993) found that tutors who were unfamiliar with the discipline at hand were ineffective as tutors, as they didn't know what kinds of questions to ask. On the other hand, there was a danger of the tutor taking over the paper if she was too familiar with the subject matter. Callaway (1993) found that tutors' knowledge and membership in the academic community gave them authority, sometimes resulting in a more directive session. Stachera (2003) found that the tutors' knowledge of writing and the writing process (they were all graduate students) allowed them to be comfortable talking about writing in the session, sometimes to the point that they took over. Seckendorf (1986) found that a tutor's knowledge of a topic (in this case, feminism) caused the tutor to steer the tutee's paper toward the tutor's concerns, even though this caused the paper to no longer meet the assignment. In Ritter's (2002) study, tutors with less knowledge about and experience with papers written by non-native speakers who were upper-level and graduate students "in disciplines outside the tutor's major" resulted in discomfort for the tutor due to lack of authority (p. 267).

Experience

We discovered in our analysis that the tutors' and tutees' status as undergraduates, graduate students and professionals sometimes influenced the tutoring session. Cardenas (2000) found that tutors with more education than their tutees had more authority in the session. Cardenas also wrote that of those she studied, that is, of the tutors who approached tutorials as collaborative events,

> one consultant brings formal training in non-directive techniques, another consultant has received extensive experience in peer-tutoring practices, two other consultants have provided training sessions for other consultants assigned to the Writing Center, and one consultant applies the training that promotes student ownership of the text and student's active learning. (p. 146)

In other words, training in writing center techniques of some sort seems to make for more collaborative tutorials. Stachera (2003) found that the graduate student tutors in her study were more knowledgeable about writing and felt comfortable talking about it. Likewise, Ritter (2002) found that "tutors with more extensive experience tend to be more flexible in their approach to meet the students' needs and vice versa" (p. 259).

Race

Race factored in tutoring sessions, but in our data, Whiteness was not likely to be commented on as a racial identity. Roswell (1992) found that "students of color sought out tutors of color" (p. 181). Cook-Gumperz (1993) related a tutoring session with an African-American woman who used features of African-American discourse such as testifying. Wolcott (1989) noticed a Black female student "actively participate in her conference from the very beginning," and another Black male student who "took many minutes of 'warming up' before becoming involved with his paper." She further noted two Hispanic students, one male and one female, "actively participated in the discussions" (p. 19). Not all studies we looked at coded participants for race, but one interesting study was Haas' (1986) study in which at least one of the dyads consisted of two Black women, and at least one other tutor was Black. Although Haas did not identify her participants by race, the dyad of Laura and Sillita talked about having African ancestry and discussed their interactions with Black dialect. It's not clear why Haas chose to ignore the issue of race in her interpretation. It was obviously important to the participants, as the topic of one tutee's paper was reggae music and its message about Africa: She and her tutor discussed this in detail. Another one of the tutoring dyads Haas described spent time discussing their relationship to the dialect of Black English. The tutor, Liese, identified herself as Black, and it is implied, although not stated, that the tutee, Evelyn, was also Black. Again, the topic of race was important to the participants and Haas left it unmentioned. The participants in most of the other studies were either White of European descent, or if their race was not coded or evident from the context, it appeared to be assumed to be White in the studies. In many studies, Asian students were classed as non-native speakers and it was their linguistic status, not their race that was deemed important. In this analysis we discuss Mexican-American and Native American students under culture because the authors of the studies that mention them conclude that culture rather than race made a difference in their tutoring sessions.

Sex

Several of the studies we analyzed were concerned with the sex of tutors and tutees. Although many called this concept *gender*, we chose to call it *sex*, since it was the biological sex of the tutor that appeared more salient in the data than any perceived gender performance. Roswell (1992) found that male tutees sought out male tutors. Hunzer (1997) surveyed tutees and found that both female and male tutees found tutors of the opposite sex "less effective" as tutors (p. 7). One of Hunzer's male participants told her that male tutors were more likely to work on grammar while female tutors were more concerned with ideas. This same participant saw his "male tutor as being more analytic and straightforward" while he saw his "female tutor as being more sensitive and caring" (p. 8). The female tutees in Hunzer's study reported that they trusted their female tutors more and felt that they were more caring and understanding of their feelings. The female tutees reported that their male tutors worked on grammar more, were more directive, and took charge of the session. In Haas' (1986) study, all the participants were female. She also found that the female-female dyad was the "predominant pattern" in the writing center that she studied (p. 50). Stachera (2003) found that male-male dyads were more physical than male-female or female-female dyads, using playful touch in greeting. Cardenas (2000) claimed that gender didn't make a difference in her study, and she went so far as to change the gender of some of the participants. Since she did this, we cannot evaluate her statement. Nicolas (2002) studied ten college writing centers in depth and found that the writing centers were staffed by more female tutors than male. In fact, only one college had an even split between male and female tutors, and two colleges reported entirely female tutoring staffs. Wolcott (1989) found that two female tutees in her study, one White and one Asian, took longer than the male students in th begin asking questions or to respond "with more than m answers" (p. 19).

Age

When age was mentioned as a factor, it was mostly in relation to older tutors (and in one case a tutee), likely because when tutors and tutees were traditional college age, there was no need to mention their age. Jordan (2003) found that one tutor in her study thought that her power as a tutor was related to her age, as being older gave her more power and took away from her status as a peer. Bell (1989b) found that tutees over age 25 were more likely to be assertive in the conference and to make sure the tutor met their needs for the session. One tutor in Bean's (1998) research said that her age (30s) enabled her to enact the comforting and nurturing tutoring style required by her writing center director. The tutors in Wolcott's (1989) study were graduate students ranging in age from their early 30s to late 40s. Their tutorials frequently got down to business without any small talk, greetings, or pleasantries. Wolcott attributes this "business-like tone" to their maturity (p. 19).

(Non-)native English Speaker

In most of the research studies we read, the tutee had the status of non-native speaker (NNS), and the tutor had the status of native speaker (NS). This is probably due to the assumption that tutors must have strong English skills and that the tutee needs help with English. These identities influence the session in a number of ways. For instance, in Thonus' (2004) study of tutoring interactions between native speakers and non-native speakers, she found that tutors used less negotiation with NNS tutees. She also found that tutors spoke more and controlled the session more, used less mitigation in directives, and asked a lot of questions rather than negotiating. Tutors took time to explain the tutoring session to the NNS, something that they didn't do with native speakers. They also frequently deflected issues to the teacher, telling the NNS student to go back and ask the teacher. Bell and Youmans (2006) found that non-native speakers sometimes misunderstood tutors' politeness strategies and took them at face value, resulting in confusion for the tutee. International students also desired the tutor to be knowledgeable and to impart that knowledge in a directive manner (Vallejo, 2004; Carter-Tod, 1995).

Thonus (2003) mentioned another kind of NNS, Generation 1.5 Learners, who are different from ESL/EFL students in that they've come up through the US educational system and have different needs than international students. Her research showed that these learners need to be guided through the procedures of the tutorial so they know what to expect from the tutor. Their cultural and linguistic heritage needs to be valued, as well as their personal identities. She also found that effective tutorials with Generation 1.5 students balanced grammar with rhetorical concerns. Like other NNS students, Generation 1.5 Learners benefit from some direction, and she showed in her data how they can become confused when tutors appeal to native speaker intuition about the English language. These students may not possess this intuition even though they appear to speak English fluently.

To these ends, our analysis showed us that the linguistic status of tutees can also influence the format of the session. In the data we examined, NNS tutees sometimes desired or required more directivity than NS tutees. Tutors who were determined to remain in a non-directive stance frustrated such tutees, resulting in guilt feelings in the tutor if she should abandon the non-directive practices advocated in training (Blau, Hall, & Sparks, 2002). Blau, Hall, Davis, and Gravitz (2001) found that native speaker tutors, in sessions with non-native speaker tutees, acted as "cultural informants" (p. 2). Blau, Hall, and Sparks (2002) also mentioned this concept and showed that it possibly helps build rapport, "increasing the collaboration between tutor and client" (p. 30), as the tutee can also share information about his or her home culture with the tutor.

Ritter (2002) found that many times native speaker tutors focused on grammar with ESL (NNS) students. This may be due to the fact that tutors with less experience felt uncomfortable tutoring ESL students, especially those who were writing upper-level papers in disciplines with which the tutor may not have been familiar. Ritter also found that tutors often made wrong assumptions about NNS tutees, such as when a tutor assumed that a graduate student was a freshman.

Cogie (2006) found a difference in negotiation between NS and NNS in the tutorials she observed. In one of the tutorials negotiation of the meanings of words was successful, while in another the negotiation of the organization and level of detail of the assignment was unsuccessful, seemingly because the tutee did not understand what the tutor was trying to communicate. Wolcott (1989) noted that many tutorials with non-native speakers in her study focused on diction, particularly idiomatic usage. Carter-Tod (1995) described a case study in which an upper-level ESL student came to the writing center with finished drafts and only wanted the tutor to help her with idiomatic English. The freshman writers in her study desired help with all aspects of the writing process, especially the rhetorical. Blau, Hall, and Sparks (2002) mentioned that many times it is useful for a tutor to go over a NNS student's paper for mechanics, even though this went against their writing center training. Their data showed that a tutoring session could weave together work on both global and local concerns. They also showed how it could be beneficial for a tutor to work line-by-line through a portion of the student's paper. Kim (2000) showed both NS and NNS tutees asked specific informational questions of their tutors, although the NNS tutees did so to a greater extent.

(Dis)ability

Both tutors and tutees can have disabilities that may influence the tutoring session, although there is little available research on tutors with disabilities. In one session that Bell (1999) observed, the tutee mentioned that she might be dyslexic and that both of her parents were as well. She resisted identifying herself as dyslexic, and the tutor said she did not understand dyslexia. This was obvious as she persisted in asking the tutee questions about her perceptions of print and then gave her sentence-combining exercises. Lerner (1996) also observed learning disabled tutees in the writing center, one diagnosed, one undiagnosed. Lerner contrasted the "free" help available in the writing center with the for-a-fee tutoring available in the disabilities services office. Babcock (2005) studied deaf tutees in the writing center. Their deafness could influence their writing skills as well as the communication methods used in the conference (the presence of an interpreter). Since 2006 (the bounds of this study) more research on disability has begun to appear. We hope this trend may continue.

Cultural Identity

Among other personal characteristics, tutors and tutees bring their cultures with them to the tutoring session. These could be either subcultures of American students or varied cultures of other cultural groups or international students. In the studies we looked at, culture came into play in the case of international students who were not familiar with American discourse conventions, especially politeness strategies and expectations (Bell & Youmans, 2006; Young, 1992). Young (1992) also found that differences in culture could result in differences in writing styles. Fox (2003), likewise, noted that culture can influence how students write. DiPardo (1992) found that culture was an influence, and the tutor in her study was not sensitive to the fact that her tutee was a Navajo, an English language learner, and an outsider to academic culture. In another study, the tutee's culture set him in opposition to the academic discourse community. In this study (Rodby, 2002), a tutee resisted the discursive position set up for him by an assignment for a course in leisure studies. Rodby suspected the tutee's status as a Mexican-American child of farm workers and grandchild of immigrants put him in a different relation to leisure than the assignment assumed. Deaf people could also be members of Deaf Culture, though not necessarily so. Because Deaf culture values directness, Deaf people could be offended or confused by the non-directive nature of the tutoring conference (Babcock, 2005).

Preparation

Preparedness was a personal characteristic that the research team identified as affecting the tutoring session in several studies. Ritter (2002) found that some tutees came to tutoring extremely prepared, with their drafts marked as to the specific questions they wanted to ask in the tutorial. Cardenas (2000) also noted a tutee who came to the session extremely prepared and that this resulted in one of the few truly student-initiated collaborative sessions in her observations. Stachera (2003) also noted a tutee who came prepared to the session with two copies of her document, showing her to be "invested" and "attentive" (p. 212). Callaway (1993) noted a tutee in her study who came to her tutoring session unprepared and apologized to the tutor for wasting her time.

Attitude

Our analysis of the studies found that tutors' and tutees' attitudes were classed as either negative or positive. Presumably, if the attitudes were neutral, they would not be worth commenting on in a study. Murphy's (2001) study found that the English department as a whole had a negative attitude toward the writing center, and that "writing center work is not held in high esteem, and has sometimes been equated with either incompetence or inability to teach. As a result, writing center work is not always valued highly by either faculty or by graduate students" (p. 37). The attitude can also change during the tutoring session. Wolcott (1989) reported that the tutors in her study felt that tutees came away from the tutoring session with improved attitudes towards writing, and that students "left [the tutoring session] with a sense of the importance of writing" (p. 24).

Writing Skills

From what we observed, the writing skills of both the tutor and the tutee can influence the session. Roswell (1992) described the relation between the tutor's and tutee's writing skills as one of master and apprentice, the "representation of the student as a writer with distinct habits or style" (p. 151), and that the only difference between tutor and tutee writing skills were "time and practice" (p. 152). Frank wrote that writing skills are a personal characteristic that can be improved or changed during the session (Frank, 1983). The tutors in Wolcott's (1989) study felt that tutees learned valuable rules in the tutoring session that they could apply to their writing in the future. Sometimes a tutee will come to the session with a disparaging attitude toward his or her own writing skills. McInereney (1998) found one such tutee in her study who was also a tutor in the writing center. This tutor/tutee chose to have her session with a less experienced tutor, possibly because she felt more comfortable exposing her writing to someone of less perceived status. Cook-Gumperz (1993) examined a tutoring session in which the writer struggled with issues of her own voice and academic discourse.

Callaway (1993) reported a tutoring dyad in which both participants considered themselves writers, but the tutee, Cassie, had been admitted to the university provisionally, so she didn't have the academic stamp of approval on her writing. Since her tutor was a writer too, there was also a sense of competition between them. The tutor considered Cassie "a very competent writer" (p. 404), but Cassie was ambivalent about the advice she was getting from her tutor. The tutor, Johanna, broke the ice when she showed Cassie some of her poems. This same tutor worked with a tutee who had very poor writing skills, and this caused Johanna frustration in the session. With Cassie, the tutor's frustration was caused by Cassie's good writing and the tutor finding no errors to correct.

Appearance

In the study data, sometimes tutors or tutees were judged and categorized by their outward appearance. The tutor, Johanna, in Callaway's (1993) study had long hair, and in this case her tutee judged her wrongly as being conservative and a Born-Again Christian. Some tutors in the studies we looked at were very aware of their outward appearance and how it influenced the session. One of the tutors in Stachera's (2003) study talked about how she altered her dress when she came to the writing center. As an older graduate student and a teacher, she would dress in "an informal top and jeans and ...tennis shoes" rather than a suit, to "make the students feel more comfortable" (p. 184). In her own experience, she said, she thought the students would feel intimidated or scared or frightened to see a doctoral student in a suit in the writing center. This hypothesis is not supported, however, because the students in the study were not asked how they felt about their tutors' dress. McClure (1990) noted a tutor who came to the writing center sometimes in slippers, sometimes barefoot, demonstrating her comfort with being in the writing center.

Summary[1]

Knowledge

- Students who identified with a particular discourse community sought out tutors within that community (Roswell, 1992).
- Knowledge of a subject gave tutors perceived power and authority during tutoring sessions, sometimes to a negative extent (Jordan, 2003; Callaway, 1993; Seckendorf, 1986; Stachera, 2003), whereas lack of knowledge created ineffective tutors (Kiedaisch & Dinitz, 1993).
- Tutors with less knowledge about and experience with non-native speakers felt a lack of authority during tutoring sessions (Ritter, 2002).

Experience

- Tutors with more education (graduate students and professionals) had more authority in tutoring sessions (Cardenas, 2000).
- Receiving training in writing center techniques assisted tutors in leading more collaborative sessions (Cardenas, 2000).
- Tutors with more education tended to be more comfortable discussing writing (Stachera, 2003) and more flexible in their approaches to tutoring (Ritter, 2002).

Race

- Students of color had a tendency to seek out tutors of color (Roswell, 1992).
- In tutoring dyads where participants were of the same race, the tutee more actively participated in the tutoring session (Wolcott, 1989).

Sex

- Tutees sought out tutors of the same gender (Roswell, 1992) and appeared to be more comfortable with tutors of the same gender (Hunzer, 1997).
- Male tutors were viewed as being analytical and taking charge of tutoring sessions (Hunzer, 1997).
- Female tutors were viewed as being sensitive and understanding (Hunzer, 1997).
- Overall, female tutors dominated the writing center staffs that were studied (Nicolas, 2002).

Age

- Older tutors, those age 25 and above, viewed themselves as having more power (Jordan, 2003).
- Older tutors also conducted more businesslike tutoring sessions (Wolcott, 1989).
- Tutees age 25 and over were more assertive and made certain that their tutoring needs were met (Bell, 1989b).

(Non-)native English Speaker

- Tutors tended to be native English speakers and took control of tutoring sessions in which the tutee was a non-native speaker (Thonus, 2004; Blau, Hall, Davis, & Gravitz, 2001).
- Non-native English speaking tutees expected tutors to be knowledgeable about the subject and to offer (directive) assistance (Vallejo, 2004; Carter-Tod, 1995).
- NNS learners benefited from direction with regard to the procedures of tutoring sessions as well as with regard to their papers (Thonus, 2003), and politeness sometimes resulted in confusion (Bell & Youmans, 2006).
- Native speaking tutors often spent time going over the mechanics of a NNS tutee's paper (Blau, Hall, & Sparks, 2002), focusing on grammar (Ritter, 2002), or words (Cogie, 2006; Wolcott, 1989; Carter-Tod, 1995).

(Dis)ability

- The disabilities of both tutors and tutees can affect the outcome of a tutoring session.
- Deaf tutees' experience in tutoring sessions could be affected by their deafness as well as by the communication methods used in the session (Babcock, 2005).

Cultural Identity

- International students were often unfamiliar with American discourse conventions (Bell & Youmans, 2006; Young, 1992).
- Culture can influence students' writing styles (Young, 1992; Fox, 2003) and their relationship to the subject (Rodby, 2002).
- Writing center training techniques such as non-directiveness may also affect students of other cultures (Babcock, 2005).

Preparation

- Prepared tutees tend to have more specific questions to ask during tutoring sessions (Ritter, 2002) and may even initiate collaboration during the session (Cardenas, 2000).

Attitude

- Departments within a university may have a negative attitude toward the writing center (Murphy, 2001).
- Students may leave the writing center with better attitudes toward writing than before the tutoring session (Wolcott, 1989).

Writing Skills

- Tutor and tutee's writing skills can be compared to that of master and apprentice (Roswell, 1992).
- Tutees sometimes come to a tutoring session with a negative attitude toward their own writing (McInerney, 1998; Cook-Gumperz, 1993), and they may seek a less experienced tutor for this reason (McInerney, 1998).

- Tutors may experience frustration with tutees whose writing skills are poor, or whose papers do not require any correction (Callaway, 1993).

Appearance

- Tutors can be judged based on their outward appearance and may change their dress to affect tutee's attitudes toward them (Stachera, 2003).
- Some tutors exhibited their comfort in the writing center environment by way of their appearance (McClure, 1990).

Note

1 These summaries are based on the results of our synthesis and are accurate according to our grounded theory analysis. We make no claim to their being generalizable to all contexts, but these are the findings as they emerged from our study. We offer them as a courtesy to the reader.

CHAPTER THREE

External Influences

The entire discourse community as a whole, and Standard English in particular, influence the tutoring session. Hemmeter and Mee (1993) pointed out that "what is in fact happening in these [writing center] interactions involves connectedness to a much broader discourse in the college community and beyond. Moreover, these interactions are affected by a variety of socially and culturally determined expectations" (p. 4). Several tutors in Jordan's (2003) study discussed the importance of the larger discourse community and Standard English as influences in the tutoring session. Other influences are the university, the discipline, the subject, the course, the instructor, the writing center director, the tutor's preparation, the cultural milieu, the genre and even the tutoring medium. These influences become even more complicated, as Roswell (1992) observed, when they are in conflict with each other. Cook-Gumperz (1993) examined a tutoring session in which the writer struggled with issues of her own voice and academic discourse; as with writing skills, external factors can exert pressure on a writer's ability to perform.

University

Universities, by definition, exist within a particular socio-cultural realm replete with its own mores and hierarchies. Academic writing must meet the standards set by the instructor, satisfactorily fulfill the assignment requirements of each course, and meet the academic rigors of the chosen discipline. Those people employed by the university are conferred with the authority or perceived authority to uphold this culture. This includes the staff of a writing center. Students matriculating at a university become enculturated to academe and perceive writing tutors as participants in and upholders of academe as noted in the works of such researchers as Lerner (1996) and Thonus (1999a). Callaway (1993) observed a student, Cassie, who appeared to be resistant to the university as a whole, and to her tutor as a representative of the academy. Callaway suggested that this was because Cassie was admitted as a provisional student and because she was Black. Cassie displayed much resentment and ambivalence in her tutoring sessions. At the same time, she wanted feedback, had lots of excuses about her writing, and sometimes insisted on not changing her text. In general, as Young (1992) noted, "A writing center is...traditionally staffed by individuals who are unusually accepting of students, however 'standard' their writing happens to be, perhaps because of their own marginal status within the academy" (p. 43).

Academic Discourse

Academic discourse is an outside influence on the tutoring session because many times students struggle to grapple with it. Oftentimes students will come to the writing center trying to negotiate the intersection of their own voice (Cook-Gumperz, 1993), or their own authority (Welch, 1995) and academic discourse.

Subject

The academic subject being studied is sometimes itself an outside influence on the tutoring session. Rodby (2002) observed a student who was quite resistant to the position that the subject (leisure studies) and his professor, through her comments on his paper, were placing him in. As a Mexican-American migrant, the discourse of recreation studies was foreign to him, which caused him to resist the assignment and the tutor's suggestions. The end result was that the tutor suggested they work on grammar. Bell (1989b) discussed a tutee who was simply intimidated by the subject matter, "swamped by philosophy" and "obsequious...to overwhelming, inscrutable philosophy" (p. 128). In another case, Murphy (2001) observed a tutor who invoked the subject of literature as an outside influence on the tutoring session. In several turns the tutor said such things as "the reason we use literary critics is because we want to say we realize that we don't have the authority to say this," and that the writer should be "standing on the authority of these other critics who've gotten published," and "that's really why we use sources" (pp. 64–65). Roswell (1992) noted the outside influence of discourse conventions on the tutoring sessions, especially in the form of mini-lessons that the tutor would offer on topics of rhetorical expectations.

Course

Since most tutees attend the writing center to get help with particular course papers, it is not surprising that the course itself exerts an influence over the session. Haas (1986) wrote about a tutee feeling unhappiness and confusion about a course. In Callaway (1993), Cassie was resistant to the assignment, to the course, and to the academy in general.

Teacher

Clearly, the teacher is a ghostly presence in the writing center tutorial, since the teacher gives the assignments and grades the papers. Blau, Hall, and Sparks (2002) wrote about native speaker tutors encouraging non-native speaker tutees to approach their teachers about any questions they had about their writing assignments, and how this may be something that students from other countries were unaccustomed to. Lerner (1996) noted a non-native speaker who preferred to consult with the teacher on matters of teacher preference (matters of content) and to consult with a tutor for matters of grammar and style, and that for all tutees, the classroom instructors were concerned with "correctness." Jordan (2003) indicated that some writing center visits were required by the teacher, and also that students often came into the writing center with texts marked by the teacher. She also mentioned that in some respects the student text is "owned" by the teacher and writing center director (p. 132). Sometimes the tutor did not explicitly focus on what the teacher wanted (p. 150), while sometimes the tutor became an agent for the teacher (pp. 152–158). Jordan also observed tutors evaluating teachers' comments, and even one case in which the tutor had to explain to the student that the teacher's comments were actually wrong (p. 176). Callaway (1993) also noticed a tutor and tutee dealing with teacher comments and expectations. As in the case that Jordan observed, the tutor in Callway's study also disagreed with the teacher's comments. In a session that Cogie (2001) observed, a graduate student tutor and first year writer attempted to negotiate the teacher's comments on the tutee's paper. The tutor in this case disagreed with the teacher's comments, but common writing center practice states that the tutor does not criticize the teacher's assignments or comments. The tutor helped the student find a way to follow the teacher's comments. In this way, the tutor tried to work between what the student wanted to do with her paper and what the teacher wanted, but in a non-directive manner.

Rodby (2002) also noted how the role of the teacher can enter the tutoring session. In the conference she observed, the student defended his paper against his teacher's comments, all the while not understanding what the teacher wanted. The tutor attempted to explain the teacher's assignment and expectations, but the student continued to resist. Severino (1992) observed a session where the teacher was an absent presence. This student brought outside pressures to the tutoring session which affected his thinking on his paper. The student, Joe, was apprehensive about the teacher, and "the teacher and the interviewee [the subject of the paper] lurk in the background affecting the session and the text, although physically they weren't present" (p. 59). Roswell (1992), too, noted the presence of the instructor as an influence in the conference. This takes place in the desire of the tutor and tutee to help the paper meet the teacher's expectations.

Johnstone (1989) found when a tutor attended a writing workshop, the tutor then based her expectations for the tutee on the expectations the workshop teachers placed on the tutor. Such expectations can work in an opposite fashion, such as Waring's study on resistance in tutoring encounters. Waring (2005) also noticed that the teacher, although not physically present, is a participant in the tutoring session. Waring (2005) suggested that tutees may resist a tutor's advice by invoking a higher authority, that of the professor for whom the writing is produced. Specifically, a tutee offered an account as to why the tutor's advice is "incongruent with the specific needs of [the] paper, thereby resisting the advice..." of the tutor by citing the professor's instructions. In this instance, the tutee attempted to trump the tutor's authority with the greater authority of the instructor. Magnotto (1991) observed students in conferences trying to write for the teacher, trying to "psych out" what the teacher wanted and being concerned with getting it right or wrong. The teacher's desires were a strong presence in the conferences that Magnotto observed for both the tutors and tutees, and it was also clear that the teacher was seen as the primary audience for writing. This was also the case in Lerner (1996). Haas noted that sometimes the tutor and tutee had "different aims, and their purposes sometimes differed from the teacher's written comments on the draft" (1986, p. 56). In particular, a tutor in this study noted that her tutee "had a lot of enthusiasm in the beginning of the term, but her teacher pounced on every little thing, so she got disappointed and regressed" (p. 116).

Director

Of course the director is an outside influence on the tutoring session, through training, selection of tutors, and the general atmosphere of the writing center. In the center where Bean (1998) did her research, the director encouraged tutors to greet students and make them comfortable. She made suggestions like

> THINK OF YOURSELF AS A...sympathetic listener...questioner...guide to resources..."dumb" (but very attentive) reader...coach.
>
> SET THE TONE BY...smiling, greeting the student at the door, learning her name and introducing yourself, offering coffee or tea, taking time for small talk, remembering the importance of eye contact and body language.
>
> SEND THE RIGHT SIGNALS BY...sitting next to the student, asking *her* to tell you as much as she can about the assignment, making sure the paper and pen are in *her* hands, reading the work in progress aloud and encourage *her* to stop at any point where *she* wants to ask questions, reflecting/restating what you hear her saying, *listening* more than you talk. (p. 134)

Female tutors in the study were more comfortable with these practices than were the males, as many of the above behaviors appear to be gendered female.

Selection of tutor. In her study of tutoring writing with deaf tutees in the writing center, Babcock (2005) investigated how tutors were selected to work with "special" populations, such as deaf students. She learned from her participants that there was a sense that a good tutor for a deaf student would be someone who knew ASL. Other qualities that administrators mentioned were "good interpersonal skills, a good tutor in 'regular criteria,' personality, and willingness to do it," also, tolerance and "someone who tutees might respond to well." Other qualities mentioned were open-mindedness, willingness to try new things, "someone 'who's willing to try something different with a different kind of student," as well as tutors who exhibited attitudes of encouragement and caring, and the ability "to change his teaching style to meet with the student's learning style" (pp. 224–225). Carter-Tod (1995) observed a tutee choosing a tutor due to their rapport with one another or due to the way they worked together. Although in this case the tutee selected the tutor, ultimately the tutee chose from the tutors that had already been "pre-selected" by the director. We understand that in some writing centers new tutors are chosen by the existing tutors, but that was not the case in the studies we analyzed.

Training. Tutor training can affect the tutoring relationship, especially when tutors are trained in one particular approach that may not jibe with the students' needs. A tutee, Cassie, mentioned this in Callaway's (1993) study. In this case, the tutee suggested that directors "prepare the tutors to be more flexible in meeting the variety of student needs. I got the impression that tutors are trained to assist a singular composite student and then with tremendous limitations imposed" (p. 577). The tutor in the study, Joanna, rigidly adhered to the expressivist tenets she learned in her training, effectively closing off other aspects of learning. The director in Bean's (1998) study trained her tutors not to evaluate or give any input or critique regarding the instructor or assignment. Cardenas (2000) saw that the type of training received influenced the type of session the tutor conducted. For instance, of those in her study who engaged in collaborative sessions,

> one consultant brings formal training in non-directive techniques, another consultant has received extensive experience in peer-tutoring practices, two other consultants have provided training sessions for other consultants assigned to the Writing Center, and one consultant applies the training that promotes student ownership of the text and student's active learning. (p. 146)

Other People

Sometimes other people are influences on the tutoring session as in the case of a tutee who had asked his sister to help with his paper and sought tutoring to give her a break (Cardenas, 2000). Another outside influence on the tutoring session is the audience that is invoked by the participants (Briggs, 1991). This audience can be real (often it is the teacher, or actual named friends and associates), or just invoked, a "general reader" or someone who would be interested in the specific text (e.g., women, people who want to improve themselves). Other outside influences that were brought into the tutoring session were other books and writers in relation to the writer's writing. This could also include the writers the student writer was using for sources. Regarding this, Briggs found that "the influence of others not visibly present in the writing center encounter constitute a web of readers—nearly transparent, yet strong enough to influence the direction of a discussion, make the writer revise a text, or irritate the participants" (pp. 55–56).

Duration of Relationship

This category has to do with both relationships that develop in the tutoring sessions and those existing outside relationships that affect the tutoring process. Though they are outside the tutoring process, these external relationships can intrude on a tutoring session. For instance, the tutor Jill (McClure, 1990) behaved very differently when a friend came into the writing center. Instead of tutoring the way she was trained, with the use of encouragement, questioning, and making suggestions, with her friend she just proofread, as that's what he wanted. She did not want to be too pushy with her agenda for the tutoring session for fear of damaging the outside relationship. In this same study a male/male dyad who were friends outside the writing center displayed a more collaborative tutoring relationship.

Sometimes it takes a while for a tutor and tutee to develop a relationship, but once they do, it may result in a more effective session. For instance, Johanna and Cassie, a tutor and tutee that Callaway (1993) described, developed a relationship with each other over several tutoring sessions. Their earlier sessions were "non-productive" according to Cassie (p. 175). Building a relationship is not the same as liking each other. Both women liked each other from the beginning, but they had not built that firm foundation of a relationship that was necessary for them to be able to work together on Cassie's paper. They went through several tutoring sessions that consisted of relationship building where all talk was seen as unproductive. In the final tutoring session of the semester, Johanna gave Cassie directive comments. At first Cassie balked, but then she accepted the direct criticism of her paper and felt the session was a success. Briggs (1991) found that the duration of the relationship influenced talk about audience other than the teacher. Roswell (1992) recorded the existing relationship between tutors and tutees, but did not indicate how these relationships influenced the session, except in the case where both participants were tutors, making them "true peers" (p. 137). These sessions were "identified as most successful by both participants."

Expectations (Tutor and Tutee)

Both tutor and tutee bring expectations with them to the tutoring sessions. Lerner (1996) observed that differing expectations from the tutoring session can result in role conflict between tutor and tutee. Particularly, he wrote, "Notions of a pure 'student centeredness' do not recognize the day-to-day influences on writing in college" (p. 35). An example of this was seen in Hunter (1993) in which a tutee, Yvonne, expected to have her paper edited, and instead the tutor asked her exam questions about "matters of punctuation and syntax," which "annoyed Yvonne further" (p. 133). Harris (1995) noted that because of expectations, people who have not been in a writing tutorial before may react negatively because they assume there will be directive instruction from the writing tutor. However, these findings suggested that the vast majority of students felt far more satisfied when they were allowed to find their own way with the guidance of a writing tutor. She wrote that it "appears that writers both need and want discussion that engages them actively with their ideas through talk and permits them to stay in control" (p. 31). Vallejo (2004) interviewed an international student who expected her tutor to be knowledgeable and have the authority to impart that knowledge. When tutors have expectations about tutees, this can influence the session, especially if the tutors don't take the time to talk to the tutees about their academic level (freshman, sophomore, graduate student, etc.), and what type of paper they are writing rather than proceeding on assumptions (Ritter, 2002). The interviews in Bean's (1999) study indicated the presence of powerful cultural beliefs about linguistic behavior and that women are more receptive, nurturing, talkative, and approachable, while men are more assertive, direct, and authoritative, and, when in the "subordinate" position of needing help, more taciturn and closed. These perceptions about language and gender influenced how consultants approached conversations in the writing center (p. 135).

Hunzer (1997) mentioned that the gender attitudes of the tutees in her survey may have been influenced by gender stereotypes they held. Similarly, tutees, especially ESL students, tended to expect directive instruction from tutors who were traditionally trained in non-directive methods (Ritter, 2002). Boudreaux (1998) mentioned expectations in her study as affecting the success and outcome of the session. She explained this as "the framework or schema or script the tutor and writer carry in their minds of what a writing conference is" (p. 79), which could be the tutor wanting to instill confidence, or the tutee wanting to correct commas. Boudreaux explained that if the tutor and writer have a "different frame of reference" (p. 80) relating to their expectations of the writing conference, this could cause disfluency, but when the tutor and writer had similar expectations, this resulted in "effortless flow of talk" and "improvement in [the tutee's] work" (p. 81). Callaway (1993) observed a tutor and tutee who had different expectations for the session, which resulted in conflict. The tutor wanted to discuss writing in general and the writing process, while the tutee wanted to get her paper fixed. Thonus (2001) found that instructor, tutor and tutee expectations of tutor and tutee roles are as varied as the individuals who hold them.

Cultural Milieu

This category deals with the surrounding culture, rather than the cultures that the individual participants bring with them to the session, which was discussed under Personal Characteristics. Most of the studies took place in a US context and involved mainstream US cultural expectations. For non-native speakers, this could be a problem. Conventional concepts of politeness, for example, came into conflict when tutor and tutee had differing cultural expectations (Young, 1992). In addition to politeness conventions, cultural influences also related to rhetorical expectations (Fox, 2003). These expectations are part of the university, and students need to understand that "the way they write is in large part culturally or educationally determined" (p. 9), and tutors can encourage tutees to "write for an American audience" without "abandoning who they are." On the other hand, Welch (1995) concluded that cultural and disciplinary conventions often become barriers for some graduate students, just as they are the accepted means of entrance into academic discourse for others. Blau, Hall, and Sparks (2002) talked about the importance of tutor as cultural informant for international students.

Physical Space

The physical space of a writing center can be an influence, especially because it can be seen as a location that holds community (McInerney, 1998). This physical place can foster belonging and relationships. Hemmeter and Mee (1993) commented on the physical space of the writing center and how "the writing center's location on campus also impacts the interactions that take place" (p. 4). Some participants in their study likened the writing center's location in the campus library as a "fishbowl" or "train station." If the physical space seems limiting or, in the previous example, uncomfortably exposing, the tutorial will necessarily be impacted. Its location and design, therefore, are important elements.

Time

Time can be an issue, especially in online tutoring, as one of the participants in Robertson's (2005) study pointed out. Although an online tutorial can take more time than a face-to-face tutorial, it does not have to. Of the four tutees in Robertson's study, one claimed that online tutoring sessions took less time, and another indicated that sometimes face-to-face tutorials can take two hours (p. 84). However, the time factor can be an advantage since the tutor is not under pressure to give an immediate response to the paper. With an online tutorial, the tutor can ruminate over the paper, return to it, and take her time to give a complete, satisfactory, and reflective response (Robertson, 2005; Moser, 2002). Sometimes students' outside commitments are an outside influence on time. For instance, in one of the sessions Callaway (1993) observed, the tutee said that time pressures at work were preventing her from attending class and having drafts to work on. This caused them to feel that they sometimes had nothing to work on in the tutoring sessions. Briggs (1991) found that when time wasn't a factor (when they weren't pressed for time), the tutoring dyad she studied could explore more personal reactions to the writing. One tutor in Lerner's (1996) study commented that one half hour was not enough time to do justice to both the paper and the tutor/tutee relationship.

Medium

The medium of the tutorial is usually on-line or face-to-face. Some researchers have noted the differences in tutoring in these different media. For instance, Robertson (2005) studied tutors' perceptions of online tutoring and found that the online environment can sometimes lessen frustration, especially when papers are submitted last-minute. This has to do with the absence of the emotional presence of the other person so the tutor can concentrate only on the paper. This creates a more text-based conference, but as one of the tutors in Robertson's study noted, "The tutor [should] just keep in mind that we are still dealing with students not just papers" (p. 68). Moser (2002) also noted differences between face-to-face and computer-mediated tutoring. Some of these are the "pressure of the other": There is less pressure when working online; tutors can go back and re-read sections of the paper as many times as they want (p. 19). Tutors have more opportunity to think through what they want to say in an on-line tutorial, and impressions are only formed through the text, not through other factors as in the face-to-face tutorial.

Summary

University

- Tutors are viewed as representatives of the university, and tutees may react positively or negatively to them as such (Callaway, 1993).
- Writing center staff are usually very accepting of students, regardless of their writing ability (Young, 1992).

Academic Discourse

- Tutees face the intersection of academic discourse and their own voice (Cook-Gumperz, 1993) and authority (Welch, 1995) in tutoring sessions.

Subject

- The academic subject can affect the tutoring session when it is foreign to the tutee (Rodby, 2002) or intimidating (Bell, 1989b).

Course

- Tutees may exhibit a range of attitudes toward the course itself, which in turn impact the tutoring session. These may include confusion and unhappiness (Haas, 1986) or resistance (Callaway, 1993).

Teacher

- Tutees may perceive that teachers are concerned with "correctness" in their papers (Lerner, 1996).
- Tutors do not necessarily focus on the teacher's requirements for the paper (Jordan, 2003), but they may assist tutees in negotiating what they want to do in light of teacher comments (Cogie, 2001), or they may disagree with the teacher's comments (Callaway, 1993; Jordan, 2003).
- A tutee's attitude toward the teacher may affect the tutoring session (Severino, 1992).
- The teacher may be an absent presence in the tutoring session (Rodby, 2002; Roswell, 1992; Waring, 2005), with tutees desiring to write for the teacher's expectations (Magnotto, 1991).

Director

- A director in one study encouraged tutors to create a comfortable environment for the tutees, and female tutors were more comfortable with these techniques than male tutors (Bean, 1998).
- Selection of tutors was based on their possessing certain interpersonal skills. It was important for tutors of special populations to possess qualities for working with those tutees (Babcock, 2005).
- Tutor training needs to be flexible in order to meet the various needs of tutees (Callaway, 1993).
- The type of training received by the tutor can influence the type of sessions they conduct (Cardenas, 2000).

Other People

- Other people, such as the audience, other books, and other writers may affect the tutoring session by changing the direction of the session or influencing revisions (Briggs, 1991; Cardenas, 2000).

Duration of Relationship

- Tutoring sessions between two friends can result in the tutor not pushing their agenda for the session, or in a more collaborative session (McClure, 1990).

- When a tutor and tutee develop a relationship, it can result in more effective sessions (Callaway, 1993).

Expectations (Tutor and Tutee)

- Expectations in a tutoring session can be varied, and differing expectations can cause conflict between tutor and tutee (Lerner, 1996).
- The majority of students are more satisfied with a session when they are allowed to write their own paper with some guidance from the tutor (Harris, 1995).
- When the tutor and tutee hold similar expectations about the session, the session will flow more easily (Boudreaux, 1998).

Cultural Milieu

- Tutors can encourage students to write for the specific culture around them while remaining true to their own style (Young, 1992).
- Conversely, outside cultures may become a barrier to students who struggle with adhering to them (Welch, 1995).

Physical Space

- The writing center's physical location and design can influence tutoring sessions by invoking a feeling of community (McInerney, 1998) or by making students feel exposed (Hemmeter & Mee, 1993).

Time

- Online tutorials allow the tutor to take more time on the paper (Robertson, 2005; Moser, 2002).
- Outside time constraints can cause issues during the tutoring session, especially when tutees have not had time to prepare their drafts for the tutorial (Callaway, 1993; Briggs, 1991).

Medium

- Online tutoring sessions can lessen pressure and frustration for both tutor and tutee (Robertson, 2005; Moser, 2002).

CHAPTER FOUR

Communication

When tutors and tutees come together in tutoring sessions, they bring their personal characteristics and outside influences and use communication both to relate interpersonally and to get the work of the session done.

Listening

In some tutoring sessions Cardenas (2000) studied, especially the unsuccessful ones, it did not appear that the consultants actually listened to the tutees. In one case, the tutor did not listen to the tutee's answer to her questions, causing her to have to ask the questions again. The opposite of listening, according to this consultant, was talking too much. Talking too much was also related to authority. When the tutor has the authority and controls the session, the consultant will talk more. In another consultation that Cardenas studied, the student wanted to work on brainstorming, but the tutor steered her into organizing the thoughts she already had when she was still just in the brainstorming stage. It is the authority of the tutor that allowed her to take over the session in a direction that is not what the tutee had in mind. Although the tutee expressed this fact, the tutor didn't pick up on it. The tutor was in control, and even though the student protested, the tutor continued on. In their final evaluation of the session, the tutor thought they were working on organization, when indeed the tutee did not have her ideas together yet and wanted to work on brainstorming. The tutee ended up seeing another consultant about the paper. The consultant admitted in reference to the session that she needed to "listen better" (Cardenas, 2000, p. 70). Seckendorf (1986) found another mismatch which occurred when the consultant was not sensitive to what the tutee wanted from the consultation and went off on her own focus, not aware of the messages that the tutee was sending about what she wanted out of the conversation.

Not all examples of listening in communication are negative. In some cases, the tutor listened effectively and in one case "help[ed] Gloria [the tutor] understand Donna's [the tutee] commitment to her subject...[to] understand Donna's needs, and it serve[d] her as a base for strategies to help Donna move toward her goals" (p. 98). Cardenas (2000) called this "active listening." In this case the tutor used "strategies that allow[ed] Donna to express herself." These strategies "include[d] paraphrasing; referring to ideas expressed previously by Donna...and [asking] questions" (p. 98). McClure (1990) described the tutors in her study as listeners, as did the tutors themselves and the students in their evaluations. One tutor, Jim, used listening to help students find ideas of what to write about. Sometimes whether or not someone is listening is not clear, as Boudreaux (1998) demonstrated. Some people have different "response types" and exhibit behavior that may be misinterpreted. For instance, in one session Boudreaux observed, a writer appeared to be paying no attention to the tutor, writing while she talked. It turned out that the writer was taking notes on what the tutor was saying. In addition, this writer looked at the tutor and gave backchannel cues only infrequently, but he was listening: He just had a different response type. This writer later asked for a different tutor, and Boudreaux suggested that difference in response styles can make for difficulty in tutoring.

Questioning

Researchers in this analysis noted different types of questions, such as open-ended, closed-ended and leading questions used in the tutoring session. Thonus (2004) found that when native speakers (NS) tutored non-native speakers (NNS), the tutors asked lots of questions rather than using negotiation techniques. Nicolas (2002) observed tutors who asked questions to draw tutees out. For instance, one tutor simply asked the tutee what she wanted to do with her paper. She also provided an example of a female tutor asking a female tutee questions that led "the [tutee] to articulate [the] problem herself" (p. 178). In another section, Nicolas gave an example of a tutee asking the tutor advice about what to do with his paper.

Stachera (2003) focused much of her study on analyzing tutors' questions. The tutors in the study were trained to use non-directive techniques, but what they ended up using were "leading questions", which were questions to which the tutors already had an answer in mind. These are in contrast to the truly non-directive question to which only the tutee has the answer. Roswell (1992) found that tutors used "test questions," questions to which the tutor already knew the answer. She said that the implication of these types of questions was that "students are unknowledgeable and that the purpose of instruction is to remedy this deficiency" (p. 150). Blau, Hall and Strauss (1998) called these same types of questions closed-ended questions. Their research suggested that tutors may use closed-ended questions as a combination of an attempt to remain non-directive—asking a question rather than just telling the tutee the information—and as a result of growing frustration with the tutee in the conference. They also identified two other types of questions: Open-ended, in which the tutor truly doesn't know the answer, and rhetorical questions, which gave information in the guise of a question.

Thonus (1999b) found tutors using more closed, tag, either/or, and leading questions with NNS tutees. Thonus noted that these types of questions limited the tutee's options for response. Bell (1989b) noticed a writing center director recommending "open-ended questions" (p. 65). This is an example of a director *training* tutors to use a certain type of communication. In his research Bell also noticed a tutor using a questioning process in which she "paraphrased in a questioning tone what the student had said. Doing so confirmed [the tutor's] understanding and prompted [the tutee] to elaborate" (p. 77). Bell also noted a tutee "[picking the tutor's] brains actively for what she wants/needs" (p. 164; brackets original). Haas (1986) found tutors using two types of questions: "Real questions" to which they truly did not know the answer, and "teacher questions" which "do call for a specific answer and are then evaluated by the questioner" (p. 290). Haas noted that the most successful questions and those most "useful in getting students to become engaged and active participants were those 'real questions' which allowed for a variety of answers." Haas also noticed one tutee asking a great many questions. These questions were important to the tutorial interaction and helped the tutor to know the tutee's concerns. In a tutorial analyzed by Fletcher (1993), the tutor used only closed-ended questions, sometimes of questionable utility, and seemed to ignore the real concerns of the tutee.

Stachera (2003) mentioned that the tutors in her study were uncomfortable with the type and amount of questions they asked the tutees. They also worried that they didn't ask "good" questions (p. 186). One strange omission from Stachera's dissertation is that she never mentioned or cited Johnsons' "Re-Evaluation of the Question as a Teaching Tool." Even though this came out in 1993, it's relevant and should have been referenced in a dissertation about questions in the writing center. Stachera went on to speculate why tutors used "leading questions," the tutors thinking (wrongly) that they were non-directive. She also pointed out that true non-directive questions were extremely rare in her data, and that "leading questions" could be dishonest and harmful. Sometimes questions became frustrating; for example, Hunter (1993) presented a case in which Yvonne, a tutee, had a clear understanding of what she wanted from the writing center. While working with Paula, a tutor, on a draft she considered close to her final draft, Yvonne simply wanted Paula to edit her paper and answer the questions she had. However, Paula attempted to resist by asking Yvonne exam questions which Yvonne did not care to answer, or had a different answer than what Paula expected. Both the tutor's and tutee's expectations were not met:

> Yvonne felt that she had not come to the writing center to be quizzed on matters of punctuation or syntax. She had come to have a tutor check over what she had written and tell her when something needed to be changed. Each exam question Paula asked annoyed Yvonne further. (p. 133)

Furthermore, Blau, Hall and Sparks (2002) noticed tutors using closed-ended questions in an attempt to draw information out of tutees that the tutees did not necessarily know. In the case they presented, a native-speaking tutor was questioning a non-native speaker about English word forms that he or she obviously did not know. This type of questioning is a waste of time as the tutee can only guess at the answer. Babcock (2005) also noticed a similar procedure happening between a hearing tutor and a deaf student. The student did not know the word the tutor was trying to suggest, so she just guessed until the tutor finally told her the right word.

The tutors in Jordan's (2003) study also acknowledged this process and observed that, by virtue of their questions, they took control and steered the direction of the conference where they wanted it to go, which was a show of power in the conference. These same tutors acknowledged that the tutees who ask questions can steer the conference in the direction they want. The tutees also asked questions when they were confused or did not understand what the tutor was talking about. In this study, people also asked questions to clarify what the other one was saying when they didn't understand. One of the tutors in Jordan's study opined that sometimes, by asking questions, the tutor can help tutees discover information they don't know they know. Furthermore, questions were considered empowering when they "lead to tutees' explorations of ideas; other times questions seemed a coaxing tool to elicit sentence-level changes from tutees" (pp. 124–125).

Praise

Bell and Youmans (2006) found that sometimes praise was misinterpreted by L2 students (English language learners, presumably international students). The researchers found that tutors used praise as a simple politeness strategy, but the tutees misinterpreted it as being genuine. The tutees were then confused when the tutor began questioning the paper that she or he had previously praised. Thonus (1999b) found tutors offering praise to native speaker tutees such as "Yeah, your writing's very good," and "If you can already write and you're a freshman, you're doing very well" (p. 258). The tutee accepted this praise with thanks. When the same tutor praised a NNS tutee, she qualified this praise by telling him he still needed work with his articles and word-order. In one study (Callaway, 1993), praise was taken as a negative in an NS-NS (native speaker-native speaker) tutorial, when a tutor said, "I think you'll do really well. I do," and the tutee responded with, "I don't want to hear you say that again. That's added pressure" (p. 145). Frank (1983) mentioned a writer needing "a lot of praise" (p. 80), but she did not give a specific example of the form this praise took. Bell (1989b) found that direct advice-giving may have served as the opposite of praise, disarming the tutee and lowering his or her confidence.

Confidence also factored in with praise in Bell's (1989b) research. He interviewed a tutor who said his tutoring technique included "building confidence, including praising the good parts of [tutees'] writing, the parts they should build on" (p. 157). This tutor further commented that "confidence builder" was his main tutoring role (p. 167). He remarked that praise was a way to build confidence and that he "made only positive comments" on students' papers. Nicholas (2002) found that tutors used praise to signal "a position of authority by approving of what [the tutee] has done" (p. 177). This praise took the specific form of "that's a good thing," and "I was going to say this is an appropriate length" (p. 176). Another instance of a tutor offering praise occurred in McInerney's study (1998) in which she observed one tutor telling the tutee she was working with, "Hang in there. It's a big job, but I'm really proud of you for even doing this. I think you're capable of it" (p. 152). McInerney characterized the tutor in this interaction as expressing "a great deal of empathy and encouragement" (pp. 153–154).

When discussing praise, Haas (1986) mentioned Goffman's "benign fabrication." In tutoring sessions, this is when a tutor offers praise to reassure a tutee. The draft doesn't necessarily deserve the praise, but it gives a platform so the student can be comfortable with revision. In the tutoring session Haas described between tutor Laura and tutee Sillita, Laura praised at length the subject of Sillita's composition: her mother. Haas suggested this could have been a "benign fabrication" with the goal of building rapport. Another tutee in Haas' study, Evelyn, reconceptualized her entire text as the result of tutor praise. Haas claimed that the praise allowed her to feel comfortable changing her entire text. According to Haas, praise did not appear to give a student a skewed version of the value of a text. Rather, it served to put the tutee at ease and then revisions could occur if the tutee was comfortable. She also noticed another tutor praising her tutee quite a bit, but these seemed more genuine than the other tutors' "benign fabrications." Seckendorf (1986) noted that praise sometimes was used by a tutor to subtly steer a tutee toward the tutor's preferred interpretation, for example, if a tutor praised ideas that were also the tutor's own. Cardenas (2000) and Nicolas (2002) both noted that in order to give praise, tutors had to hold the authority that put them in a position to be able to offer such an evaluation. Praise can also take the form of encouragement. Both Jill and Jim, tutors in McClure's (1990) study, encouraged their tutees. Tutors in Bell's study (1989b) also encouraged their tutees.

Negotiation

Cogie's research (2006) was with NES (native English speaking) tutors and NNS (non-native speaking) tutees. Cogie found that there was negotiation of meaning between tutors and tutees. In the two examples she gave, the first session focused on negotiation of the meaning of words and word choices, presumably because the NNS did not know the precise meaning of the English words or was unfamiliar with their use and connotation. In the second example, the tutor tried to negotiate the organization of the paper and the need for details and examples. The tutor also attempted to find out the reason for the assignment and the field trip it was based on. This negotiation was not as successful as the tutee did not seem to understand what the tutor was getting at.

Thonus (1998), in a study that included both native and non-native tutees, found that negotiation was used by the tutee to ultimately accept or reject the tutor's evaluation or suggestion. Thonus (1999b) found NS tutors and NNS tutees negotiating the focus of the tutoring session and specific changes to the paper, although sometimes the tutor would bring up a concern that the writer did not mention. Ritter (2002) observed NS tutors negotiating with NNS tutees around the meanings they attempted to convey with their papers. The techniques she saw were the confirmation check, where the tutor makes sure she has understood correctly, and the clarification request, in which the tutor has not understood and asks the student for clarification. The confirmation check can be used to negotiate words and their meanings, similar to what Cogie (2006) observed.

Laughter

In some of the studies we analyzed, tutors and tutees used humor and laughter to communicate. In some cases, such as those Thonus observed (1998), laughter helped make criticism (whether from self or another) easier to accept. It served as padding for emotional blows that could accompany the criticism. This occurred most frequently with tutees who strove for a high level of achievement, and in tutoring sessions in which the tutor and tutee had very different levels of knowledge of a subject. Thonus also found that laughter sometimes signaled embarrassment, and sometimes stood for a conversational turn. Stachera (2003) noted a tutor joking around with a tutee, putting her at ease. Ritter (2002) noticed a tutor introducing herself and then laughing, and concluded this "may have been an attempt to establish solidarity or even tone down the institutional nature of the W[riting] C[enter] T[utorial]" (p. 228). Haas (1986) noted participants in her study approached the conference in a playful way, enhancing their relationship. Boudreaux (1998) found that laughter could signal rapport, and it could also be used to diffuse awkwardness, such when asking for a favor or asking personal information. Tutors and tutees in McClure's (1990) study laughed when they were at ease or when they were especially pleased that they came up with a satisfactory solution to a problem.

Connectedness

Our analysis showed us that tutors and tutees use communication to connect to each other and form a relationship. Melnick (1984) talked about "membershipping," which is a form of talk through which tutors and tutees "share varying degrees of intellectual and social belonging in a conversation" (p. 10). Symmetrical talk, which often begins with membershipping, can also curtail the tutoring process because it may cut off the thinking of the writer. Although this membershipping and relationship building may help the student become more comfortable, carrying the steps too far may actually cause the session to lose its focus—that of helping the student—and cause it to become a personal conversation.

Bean (1998) wrote about the director encouraging tutors to relate to the tutees to make them comfortable. She criticized these behaviors as "talking like a lady" (p. 135). Callaway (1993) presented a tutoring dyad in which the tutor invited the tutee "to talk about her writing before the two ha[d] established a firm grounding to support a peer relationship" (p. 115). Calloway noted the importance of developing this relationship because before it was developed, the tutoring interaction seemed unproductive. Nicolas (2002) reported that the writing center caters to "connected learners." Online tutors in Moser's (2002) study used several features in their writing to connect to students, such as informal style, tone, emoticons, punctuation and personality discourse, which is limited disclosure of personal details.

Discourse Features

The following discourse features are mentioned in the research we analyzed as being relevant to the tutoring process.

Echoing. Blau, Hall and Strauss (1998) found that tutors used an *echoing* technique in which they would pick up on the students' use of language such as discourse markers, syntactic patterns, and playful use of language. They stated that echoing seemed to reflect—or create—an affirmation of understanding between a tutor and a client: "In all the examples that we examined, echoing occurred in sessions where the client and tutor seemed to be on the same wavelength, working together in an easy camaraderie" (p. 32). Haas (1986) noticed tutors and tutees playfully echoing each other, and she described a tutor and tutee establishing rapport and "affirm[ing] their relationship" by ritualistically using "OK" (p. 223).

Qualifying. Blau, Hall and Strauss (1998) identified *qualifying* as a discourse feature that tutors used when tension rose in the session, when tutors were attempting to be non-directive, as pause fillers, and to soften criticism. Types of qualifiers they mentioned were "comments modified by qualifying phrases or words," for instance, "first person qualifiers" like "I guess," "second person qualifiers" like "you might," and "objective voice qualifiers" like "a little" (p. 33). Thonus (1998) listed several qualifiers from Indirect (Mitigated): "Maybe the thesis doesn't have to say everything..." to Imperative: "...think about that..." (p. 90) and linguistic mitigation strategies like hedges and grammatical markers (tense, mood) that tutors used seemingly for politeness and to soften the directiveness of their talk. Ritter (2002) also noticed tutors in her study using first- and second-person modals such as "I'd put an S on checklists" and "you wanna make that plural" (p. 141). She categorized these on a scale similar to the one Thonus (1998) used of illocutionary force from least to most direct. The first- and second-person modals fell in the middle of the scale, with the least direct being the indirect suggestion and the most direct being the imperative. Ritter claimed that these discourse features were used to enhance solidarity.

Small talk. Frank (1983) wrote about the value of *small talk* and mentioned that "We may spend a whole lab session talking about [the tutee's] interests, family, or life experiences" (p. 77). Small talk can also help with topic generation, such as a student Frank mentioned whom she helped "develop prewriting strategies by getting him to talk about his interests and life at Tech" (p. 78). Haas (1986) found that tutors and tutees spent lots of time talking about particular, seemingly insignificant issues, therefore building their relationship. Wolcott (1989) studied graduate student tutors who were experienced teachers. She found there was no small talk to begin the session. The term she and the tutors used was "business-like" (p. 19) and "task-oriented" (p. 25). Hunter (1993) called small talk "talk-off-task." She noticed that the tutee, Yvonne, and her tutors were not afraid to "talk-off-task." The tutors were always able to guide the conversation back to the written work, unless Yvonne felt she was done working on her paper. Yvonne then used the talking-off-task to gain information about college life:

> Talk-off-task has the obvious advantage of interspersing the difficult work of writing and revising with pleasant, human exchanges. It also has the less obvious advantages of making the writer feel more comfort-

> able in college and helping her navigate in her academic and personal lives as she gains confidence in her abilities. (pp. 207–208)

Ritter (2002) noticed NS tutors reluctant to engage in small talk with NNS tutees because of the discomfort they felt working with these writers. Thonus (1998) did not notice small talk in all the tutorials she observed, perhaps because of the institutional nature of the tutorial discourse; but when small talk did occur, it most often came at the end of the tutorial, and according to one of the students in her study, served as a way to relax at the end of the session. Thonus found that sessions containing small talk were more likely to be highly rated by participants and lower-rated sessions did not contain small talk. However, the content of small talk and status of participants must be shared in order to result in success. Cardenas (2000) explained that in one successful tutorial she observed, participants spoke of personal topics, and this added to the "friendly, interactive environment" in the tutorial (p. 113).

Pronouns. Moser (2002) discussed the use of pronouns in online tutors' responses as being inclusive (we), more distant (I), very distant (no pronoun) or intimate, where names and other intimacy markers were used. Murphy (2001) found that tutors' use of pronouns as a discourse feature related to their authority in relation to the tutee and the discipline. For instance, when a tutor switched back and forth from "you" to "I" to "we," it indicated the tutor's "desire to both claim and reject the authority that comes with her role as graduate student, teacher, and consultant" (p. 65). Cogie (2001) noticed a tutor often framing his comments with the use of the third person plural: "We're thinking where the paper is going" (p. 43), and "One way we might do this" (p. 44), and "we have to find a way" (pp. 42–43). Perhaps this was a way to show solidarity and perhaps collaboration in the conference. In Babcock's (2005) study, she often observed tutors using the second person pronoun to tell students things like, "You need to add more" (p. 217), and "You've gotta make it plural" (p. 216). One tutor in particular used "we" to indicate shared ownership: "Here I think we should say..." (p. 217). Many times tutors used the first person to indicate their opinion: One tutor commented "I would say..." (p. 215), leaving the tutee to accept his suggestion or not.

The use of pronouns is very indicative of the relationship of tutor and tutee to the content and authority/ownership in the session.

Non-verbal

Non-verbal communication emerged as an important type of communication in our analysis. McInerney (1998) found that in the writing center she studied there was much physical closeness, which mirrored the community and family aspect of the writing center. McInerney witnessed a tutor giving another a massage, lots of

> hugs—encouraging touches on the arm, pats on the back, leaning over shoulders to read, even sharing a chair at a computer—a physical proximity that would not be customary or even possible in the classroom. Tutors put their feet on a student's chair as they converse, entering a space typically claimed as personal in North American culture. It seems, from observing, that this moving-in behavior is neither proprietary or rude, but another way of creating a connection with a student, including that student in the close physical embrace of the Center. (pp. 198–199)

She also noticed tutors being sensitive to a tutee's body language, such as the tutor who was observed working with a frustrated student who "fold[ed] her arms and squirm[ed] around." This gave the observer the impression that the student "was uneasy and didn't know how to fix their paper." The tutor got this "apathetic student motivated" by "getting the student to explain more what she meant" (p. 158). Another researcher noticed a disjunction between body language and the tutee's conception of self. Cardenas (2000) noticed a tutee who appeared reluctant, looking down at her paper. However, this tutee described herself as "assertive, outgoing." Cardenas mentioned that the tutor had been this student's former classroom teacher and that perhaps she lacked confidence in the subject and "wishe[d] to defer to the expertise of her former teacher" (pp. 79–80). McClure (1990) also noticed tutors not picking up on students' body language, getting into the draft to the point where students withdrew and gave minimal answers, signaling "growing inattention as well as dissatisfaction. The student writers no longer bent over their drafts and even pushed their chairs away from the table" (p. 155). Stachera

(2003) noticed a tutee whose body language suggested "engagement":

> She leaned into the table, rather than away, she followed along on one of two copies of her paper she brought ... she held a pencil as Kyle read...and her overall stance sent the message that she was attentive to the task at hand. (p. 212)

Stachera also noticed non-verbal communication in the form of greeting exchanges between male tutors and tutees in which she saw them "hitting each other on the arms or slapping each other's hands together when they met for the first time" (p. 110). She did not notice this with male-female or female-female dyads.

Boudreaux (1998) specifically studied nonverbal behavior in tutoring sessions. She noted that many times a "disfluency" between the two correlated with a difference in nonverbal communication style. She didn't attempt to conclude that the nonverbal communication created a successful or unsuccessful session, because it could be that the nonverbal behavior was a result of the two not clicking. Boudreaux found that eye gaze was an important indicator of "harmony" or "disfluency" in the tutoring session, although she mused that the difference or similarity in the use of eye gaze could be a contributing factor, "while the difference in gender and background of the participants may cause the particular nonverbal behavior" (p. 100). One dyad, Eleanor (tutor) and Brad (tutee), looked at each other infrequently, while another dyad, Eleanor (tutor) and Callie (tutee), frequently looked at the same thing, whether it was each other, the paper, or away. Brad's lack of eye gaze and back channeling caused Eleanor to monologue, or talk on and on, but with Callie, their talk was well-balanced.

Boudreaux said that simultaneous eye gaze, whether at each other or at the paper, is indicative of rapport. She indicated the possibility that their similar age and gender could cause them to have similar nonverbal styles. Boudreaux wrote of one tutor who used her eye gaze and facial expression to keep the writer on the topic. If the writer strayed too far from the topic, the tutor looked at the writer and stopped smiling or talking. This technique was effective. In all, Boudreaux found that similarity or difference in nonverbal communication style could be a predictor of the success of the tutoring session. Obviously, nonverbal communication is missing in the online tutoring environment (Robertson, 2005).

Summary

Listening

- Tutors and tutees both use different listening styles. Active listening is preferable; other active behaviors, such as note taking, are also beneficial even though they may be misinterpreted as disinterest (Boudreaux, 1998).
- Tutors can fail to listen; they may talk too much and overpower the tutee, dominating the session to their own ends (Cardenas, 2000).

Questioning

- Leading questioning can take the place of subtler non-directive techniques (Statchera, 2003).
- Tutors use "test questions" to gauge the responsiveness and knowledge of tutees (Roswell, 1992).
- Closed-ended questions are of the same kind as test questions and are used to convey information to tutees without being directive (Blau, Hall, and Strauss, 1998).
- Closed-ended questions limited the range of the tutee's responses and were used more frequently with NNS tutees (Thonus, 1999b).
- True non-directive questioning is rare. The broader two categories in which questions fall are "real questions" to which the tutor does not know the answer and "teacher questions" that are designed to elicit an expected answer (Haas, 1986).
- Leading questions can be dishonest and harmful (Hunter, 1993).
- Tutees can take charge of the session if they ask questions that steer the conference in the direction they need it to go (Jordan, 2003).

Praise

- Praise is used as a politeness strategy but can be misinterpreted; L2 students took their tutors' praise to be genuine and did not understand why the tutor went on to critique their papers (Bell & Youmans, 2006).
- Native speakers could also misinterpret praise due to varying levels of confidence and working condition preferences. A student rejected praise because it "added pressure" (Callaway, 1993).
- Praise can build confidence and make tutees more conscious of their abilities (Bell, 1989b).
- Praise can signal authority by implying that the tutor can withhold approval (Nicholas, 2002).
- Praise can also be used to encourage and to express empathy (McInerney, 1998).
- Praise is a "benign fabrication" that tutors use to establish confidence in tutees before they risk undermining it by discussing revision (Haas, 1986).

Negotiation

- Negotiating the meaning of words between tutors and tutees is important for both NNS and native English speaking tutees. Word choice impacts usage and connotation (Cogie, 2006).
- Tutees use negotiation to accept or reject the tutor's suggestions (Thonus, 1998).
- Tutors use confirmation checking to allow tutees to clarify what they mean (Ritter, 2002).

Laughter

- Laughter makes criticism easier to accept (Thonus, 1998).
- Laughter can signal embarrassment or a change in the conversation (Statchera, 2003).
- Laughter can lighten the atmosphere (Ritter, 2002), establish solidarity (Haas, 1986) and enhance the tutor-tutee relationship by diffusing awkwardness (Boudreax, 1998).

Connectedness

- "Membershipping" establishes intellectual and social belonging between tutor and tutee through symmetrical talk. However, this relationship-building activity may cause the session to lose focus (Melnick, 1984).
- Developing a relationship helps productivity (Bean, 1998).

Discourse Features

- Tutors and tutees employ a variety of (mostly unconscious) linguistic strategies to connect or identify with each other.
- Tutors pick up on tutees' syntactic patterns and playful use of language in order to create affirmation and understanding; it is a sign that the dyad is able to work together easily (Blau, Hall, & Strauss, 1998).
- Qualifying can indicate tension and constitutes the use of phrases like "I guess" and "you might." Tutors employ qualifying to soften criticism and to appear non-directive (Thonus, 1998).
- Qualifying can also increase solidarity when it does not indicate tension (Ritter, 2002).
- Talk about the tutee's interests, family, or life experiences can help with topic generation and building camaraderie (Frank, 1983).
- Tutees learn about more than writing from small talk and can use the information they gain to help integrate themselves into the college environment (Hunter, 1993).
- Lack of small talk can indicate discomfort. Tutors did not often engage in small talk with NNS tutees (Ritter, 2002).
- Sessions in which small talk occurred were more likely to be rated favorably by participants (Thonus, 1998).
- Changing pronouns can include a tutor as part of the university system (ex. "we") and confer authority or can help a tutor disown authority in order to achieve peerness (Murphy, 2001).
- Pronouns can be used to include the tutor and tutee as part of the same unit, therefore indicating a move toward identification or shared ownership (Babcock, 2005).

Non-verbal

- Physical closeness in the writing center can translate to physical contact—leaning over shoulders, sharing computers, etc. in ways that are not customary in classrooms (McInerney, 1998).
- Body language and its vagaries come into play in the tutorial session. Tutee's descriptions of themselves can contradict impressions of their appearances (Cardenas, 2000).
- Body language can suggest engagement (Statchera, 2003).
- Eye contact and simultaneous looking can indicate rapport and concentration (Boudreaux, 1998).
- Non-verbal communication is missing in the online tutoring environment (Robertson, 2005).

CHAPTER FIVE

Roles

Roles abound in human behavior, and the tutor and tutee can be seen as performing various roles in tutoring sessions. These roles are mostly consciously chosen. Those that are natural to the individual we consider under Personal Characteristics or Temperament. Cardenas (2000) suggested that training may influence the roles tutors take on. Boudreaux (1998) suggested that unsuccessful sessions resulted when the tutor and tutee choose conflicting roles. Similarly, Mackiewicz (2001) found that success occurred when tutor and tutee were able to negotiate complementary roles.

Other scholars have developed role categories that have informed our analysis here. Murphy (2006) proposed the categories of self-presentation of tutors along an authoritarian/non-authoritarian continuum of Expert, Educated-but-Confused Reader, Uninformed Consultant and Consultant Authority of English. Haas (1986) categorized the possible roles of tutors as Collaborator, Guardian, Initiator, Interested Reader and Teacher/Expert. The tutees' roles were Author, Client, Collaborator, Initiator and Student. The roles that we have identified are those that grew out of our continuing grounded theory analysis. In all, there seems to be a split between the aggressor, director, teacher, suggestion giver, authority on one hand; and the passive, student, listener and (perhaps) resistor, on the other.

(Non-)direct

Several sources mentioned the inappropriateness of the non-directive role when working with non-native speakers (Thonus, 1999b; Thonus, 2003; Blau, Hall & Strauss, 1998; Blau, Hall & Sparks, 2002; DiPardo, 1992). Thonus (1999b) noted that NNS can become confused when they don't understand the directiveness of the tutor's utterance. However, Thonus (1999a) found that indirect suggestions were used by both male and female tutees with both native speaker and non-native speaker tutees. Vallejo (2004) found that tutors moved along a continuum between directive and non-directive tutoring with ESL students depending upon the topic. Local issues of grammar were dealt with directively, while a nondirective approach was used for global issues. Ritter (2002) noted an unsuccessful use of non-directiveness when a tutee, instead of rejecting the tutor's inappropriate suggestions, just agreed with them or remained quiet instead of arguing with the tutor. Many times a passive tutee brought out the directiveness in the tutor. Ritter (2002) noted six kinds of "suggestion types" (p. 141) in her study. These were indirect suggestion, interrogative, first-person and second-person modals, repair and imperative. (The last two are direct, and the first- and second-person modals are close to being direct.) While one of the tutors in Bean's study (1999) found that students exerted pressure on him "to provide sufficient and authoritative instruction," another tutor viewed the directive approach "as a choice consultants make when they want to move the session along quickly" (p. 135).

The act of taking charge in the session and performing a line-by-line focus on grammar can be seen as a cop out for tutors when they want to see the session end quickly because focusing on concepts and engaging the tutee takes greater energy. Another tutor in Bean's study saw the focus on grammar sometimes associated with directive tutoring as an accommodation and choice on the tutor's part to the preferences of the tutee. The tutors in Vallejo's study (2004) moved along a continuum from directive (for local issues) to nondirective (for global issues). Vallejo pointed out that the reality in this case differs from the ideal put forth in most writing center materials that "writing centers use the collaborative/nondirective approach to assist all students" (p. 115).

Tutors in Jordan's study (2003) found non-directiveness to be more empowering for the tutees, but that sometimes some direction was needed. Again it appeared to be the tutor's decision how much directiveness was appropriate. Sometimes extreme non-directiveness on the part of the tutor could result in frustration for the tutee, especially when the tutor had an opinion that was suppressed in the name of a non-directive stance. Stachera (2003) also found that the non-direct role could sometimes be seen as dishonest, especially when the tutor did not tell the writer what she really thought about the paper. At other times, an extreme directive role could serve to disarm the tutee and shut down participation (Bell, 1989b). And, as Seckendorf (1986) noted, sometimes the tutor took a directive role and steered the paper in a different direction than the writer had intended.

(Non-)confrontational

Our analysis showed that sometimes tutors and tutees chose roles that were openly or tacitly confrontational or non-confrontational. Alexis, a tutor in McClure's study (1990), often challenged her tutees on the logic and content of their papers. When one student continually rejected her suggestions for using clearer words, she finally lost her temper and said, "OK. You write it the way you want it" (p. 129). Babcock (2005) found that one of her dyads seemed to have a confrontational relationship, as they would go back and forth, almost bickering, but the tutee reported that their relationship was good, and the tutor said they "worked quite well together" (p. 208). Seckendorf (1986) found that the desire to avoid conflict could result in a less-than-satisfactory tutoring relationship or in the tutor going in a different direction than the writer intended.

Taking Charge

Our category of taking charge includes taking control of the session and attendant active and passive roles. Fletcher (1993) found that the tutor took control of the session by asking closed-ended questions and following his own agenda rather than the tutee's. Wolcott (1989) noted that the tutors in her study ended up taking charge of the sessions, usually by asking questions. McClure (1990) studied tutors who had no formal training. She observed that "the more passively the student behaved, the more prescriptive the tutor behaved or the more the tutor controlled the conference" (p. 171). This could result in conflict, such as when a tutor and tutee disagreed about what they should be working on.

In these cases, the tutors would "ignore the student writers' attempts to direct the conference" (p. 150).

Tutors in Bell's study (1989b) were trained to reject an authoritative, teacherly role. One tutor in the study, Cleo, was unhappy with her tutoring style; she felt she was being bossy and later reflected that the students she tutored were "uninvolved and ... very withdrawn and quiet" (p. 113). Bell also noted that tutors did not have the authority to "maintain or dictate a particular [tutoring] approach when students asserted their desire for a different one" (p. 199). Thonus (2004) found that native speaking (NS) tutors took charge more and used less negotiation with non-native speaking (NNS) tutees, in addition to talking more, using less mitigation and asking many questions. One of the tutors in Jordan's study (2003) used the metaphor of driving a car to describe taking charge in the tutoring session. Letting the tutee "drive" is more empowering, yet it may be more efficient to let the tutor drive, except in the case where the tutor has the wrong idea about what the paper should be about. Such was the case in the tutoring dyad of Joan and Nancy (Seckendorf, 1986): The tutor Joan steered the paper and the conference toward her own ideas, which were not only different from the tutee's, but Joan's input didn't even meet the assignment.

Active/Passive

We discovered in our analysis that the active/passive roles are sometimes directly connected to taking charge. The active participant is the one who takes charge of the session. For Bell (1989b), passivity in the tutee brought out directivity in the tutor. One of the tutors in Jordan's study (2003) noted that the tutee had the power to sit back and be passive in the conference, manipulating the tutor to do more work. The tutors in Wolcott's study (1989) found tutees to be passive, and tutors found themselves directing the conferences, usually with questions. Tutors thought tutees viewed them as "experts, if not as actual authority figures" (p. 21). Aggression, in a positive sense, could also be seen as the opposite of passivity. McInerney (1998) wrote about a tutor who characterized the tutoring relationship as "caring and aggressive (but not intimidating!)" (p. 157). This kind of aggression is a positive, active stance, with its opposite being passivity or indifference.

McClure (1990) observed that one of the tutors in her study, Ann, found it easy to take over the conference with a passive writer, but when working with a confident student writer, she "let him share control of the conference" (p. 58). It's interesting to note that the tutor used the word "let," implying that she had the ultimate power over how much control the tutee actually had in the conference. McClure found that "the more passively the student writer behaved, the more prescriptive the tutor became or the more the tutor controlled the conference" (p. 172). One of the tutees in Seckendorf's study (1986) had to rethink her passive role in relation to the tutor. As their tutoring sessions progressed, the tutee seemed to "psych out" the tutor's stance and adjust accordingly.

The other dyad in Seckendorf's study seemed to be permanently at odds to the point where the tutee seemed to "give up" and just go along with the tutor's ideas, although they differed from her own plans for the paper. Ritter (2002) noted a successful use of passivity when a tutee, instead of outwardly rejecting a tutor's inappropriate suggestions, just agreed with them or remained quiet instead of arguing with the tutor. In the end, the student used her own ideas and rejected the tutor's suggestions; she simply did not do this in front of the tutor. Sometimes the roles in a tutoring session can carry over from other known roles, such as the dyad that Cardenas (2000) described in which a tutee took on a more passive role when tutored by her former classroom teacher. In another case in this same study, the tutee took on a passive role, while the tutor did most of the work for the session.

(Non-)authoritarian

Bell (1989b) saw passivity and authority as roles or stances, but our analysis lead us to see authority as something real, while being authoritarian or non-authoritarian as roles that people can take on. The authoritarian role sometimes comes from outside the student, as exemplified in Murphy's study (2001) in which a tutor called on the discourse community of scholars to justify what "we" do when "we" use sources in literary criticism (pp. 64–65). Sometimes one participant will cast another in an authority or compliant role, as Roswell (1992) found. In her study it was the tutor in the role of "hunched-shouldered authority" and the tutee in the role of "active compliance" (pp. v–vi). Roswell also mentioned tutors attempting to create a "conversational atmosphere" and "an informal dialogue with the tutee" (pp. 112–113). A stance of authority is also taken as a position from which to give praise and advice (McClure, 1990). However, this role can backfire, as tutors can take the stance of authority to negatively evaluate a paper, sometimes hurting the tutee's feelings (Cardenas, 2000).

Cardenas also noted instances of the tutee taking on the role of authority, such as when the tutee is the expert in the topic, or the tutee is extremely prepared and knows what he or she wants to work on. But tutors will be hesitant to take on an authoritarian role if they are not confident with the subject matter or type of student they are tutoring (Ritter, 2002), or they will direct the conference toward matters they are more comfortable dealing with, such as grammar. Bell (1989b) contrasted "the authoritative stance and the passive stance" (p. 212), but he described a tutoring session in which the tutor "seemed quite happy to let [the tutee] take the initiative, and he was careful about his role as an authority" (p. 158). Bean (1998) found that a focus on grammar actually created an authoritarian role for the tutor.

"Gendered" Approach

Sometimes a tutor will take a stance related to gender roles. This is different from *sex* (a Personal Characteristic) because people can and do take on gender roles that may or may not correspond to biological sex. Woolbright (1992) studied a tutor who attempted to take a feminist stance to tutoring, but this role conflicted with the authority that she tried to exert to get the tutee to consider her feminist interpretation. Seckendorf (1986) noted almost the same thing: A tutor desired for the student to change her arguments to the tutor's own feminist interpretation. Further relations between authority and gender were shown in Bean's 1998 study. Male tutors were uncomfortable with the feminized gender role created by the director for the tutors and struggled with this position. Another gendered approach a tutor took, or was ascribed by a tutee, was the "mother" role, especially when giving direction (Callaway, 1993). It is interesting to note, also, that there was no corresponding "father" role in any of the studies we looked at. Cardenas (2000) claimed that gender was not a factor and did not make a difference in tutorials. But since she changed the gender of her participants in the study, this claim cannot be evaluated.

Nicolas (2002) discussed the feminine "ethic of care" at work in writing center tutorials. This results in nurturing and a non-directive, non-confrontational style. A masculine style would be direct and concerned with establishing authority. Nicolas showed that both these types of tutoring interactions happen in the writing center. Nicolas also explained that the writing center literature devalues the masculine (direct, authoritative). Nicolas described a "feminine" tutoring style where the tutor didn't try to "one-up" the tutee, but simply asked for information (female-female dyad; p. 177). She also noted a male-male dyad where there was more of a struggle for authority (p.179). In her conclusion, Nicolas suggested, "We need to move our discussions of tutoring away from the directive/non-directive debate that has served to code our pedagogical practices as feminine."

Power

Jordan (2003) found that tutors exercised their power by asking questions. Tutors controlled the topics and types of questions. And one tutor in her study noted that even by encouraging tutees to have power in the conference, the tutor exerted an act of power. Nevertheless, tutees had the ultimate power over their text, as they could choose to make or ignore the suggested changes. Tutors mentioned that their power came from their position, their experience, their knowledge and their age. Vallejo (2004) found that power switched from the tutee to the tutor when the tutee's concern—grammar—was addressed in the session. Bean (1998) found that male tutors attempted to create a balance of power in the tutoring session by striving for equality, while Haas (1986) suggested that tutors should be aware of the power and control that they wield in sessions and tutor training should address that.

Resistance

Resistance is noted usually on the part of the tutee resisting the tutor's suggestions or choice of focus. Waring (2005) studied tutorials with graduate students. In one example the tutee strongly resisted the tutor's concern with punctuation and also resisted the tutor's ideas for the development and organization of her paper. This empowerment to resist could come from the fact that the tutee was paying for the service or that she was a graduate student like her tutor. Waring offered the suggestion that the tutor could find out the tutee's concerns in advance to minimize wasted time dealing with concerns that were not important to the tutee. Rodby (2002) observed a tutoring session in which the tutee was extremely resistant to the teacher's comments on his paper and the tutor's ideas and suggestions. Finally, the tutor gave up and said, "Let's work on spelling and stuff" (p. 226). Resistance became apparent in Seckendorf's (1986) study when the tutor and tutee were seemingly at odds with what they desired for the session. While the tutor would discuss text-level concerns, the tutee insisted on concentrating on sentence-level changes. Rather than giving in to discord, however, the dyad was able to work through their differences to create successful sessions.

Teacher/Peer

Tutoring roles can also fall on a continuum of teacher/peer as we found in our synthesis work. Haas (1986) observed a tutoring dyad who played at the roles of teacher/student in the conference by exaggerating them. Roswell (1992) found that tutors had to work extremely hard to cultivate the role of peer. As one tutor in her study commented, "It's hard to be a tutor, because you're just like everybody else, except no one expects you to be" (p. 85). But related to the role of teacher/peer is the role of "writer" that some tutees cast themselves in. This can be seen as the role of "master and apprentice, implying that only time and practice separate the two" (pp. 151–152). When working with international students,

Blau, Hall, Davis and Gravitz (2001) saw tutors acting in a role of "linguistic informant" rather than teacher or peer. One tutor in Bell's study (1989b) tried to be "an equal, a peer, not an authority figure" (p. 114), but he knew that this was not necessarily the case: He knew he was "in charge." A graduate student tutee in Carter-Tod's (1995) study sought and appreciated a peer relationship with her tutor.

Ritter (2002) analyzed a tutoring session in which the tutor took on the role of teacher, telling the student what to do while the student listened. This was out of character with the tutor's style in the other sessions that Ritter observed. In fact, the student in this tutorial asked specific questions for help and explanations on how to write a paper; for instance, the student specifically asked for an explanation of what parts the paper should have and mentioned by name the introduction, body, conclusion, and bibliography. So, in this case the tutor took on a teacherly role, but it was in response to a student's specific request for information. Briggs (1991) found that tutors were more likely to take on a teacherly role in short-term tutoring relationships, and the possibility to become more of a counselor or a friend was reserved for a long-term consulting relationship like the one she studied. Seckendorf (1986) observed a dyad with a typical student-teacher relationship. The tutor, Sam, was a teacher who also worked in the writing center.

(In)sincerity

Sincerity and insincerity are related to honesty and dishonesty in our framework. Stachera (2003) wrote of a conference that she had in which she was not honest about what she felt about the tutee's paper. In the name of non-directivity, she kept her negative evaluations to herself and told him that the paper was "interesting" (p. 247). She noted that non-directivity does not foster true rapport because one party is holding back, and in Stachera's case she felt this was dishonest. In Jordan's study (2003) a tutor described being deceitful and withholding information from a tutee (p. 152). The tutor had taken the same class with the same teacher and knew what the paper should be about, but withheld her knowledge to let the tutee "be an expert on the plot, on the book, as much as she knew, and just try and keep guiding her" (p. 152). McClure (1990) observed a tutor, Jill, who was honest with the tutee when she didn't understand the draft.

Summary

- Roles are consciously chosen behaviors that may be influenced by training. Unsuccessful sessions result when tutors and tutees adopt conflicting roles and success may occur when dyads negotiate complementary roles (Cardenas, 2000; Boudreaux, 1998; Mackiewicz, 2001).
- Other researchers have developed role categories, but those we present here grew out of our grounded theory analysis.

(Non-)direct

- Many sources have mentioned the inappropriateness of non-directive roles when working with NNS students. Nevertheless, tutors move along a continuum between directive and non-directive with ESL students depending on the topic at hand (Vallejo, 2004).
- Non-directiveness fails when tutees agree with the tutor or remain quiet instead of defending against unhelpful or inappropriate suggestions (Ritter, 2002).
- A passive tutee can create a directive tutor (Ritter, 2002).
- Focusing on grammar can be both an acquiescence to the tutee's needs and a method of avoiding engaging with the tutee and addressing his or her needs (Bean, 1999).
- Non-directiveness can be empowering, but it must not be used to the extent that it frustrates the tutee or prevents the tutor from being honest (Statchera, 2003).

(Non-)confrontational

- Tutors and tutees can appear to be bickering, and this situation can be both productive and unproductive (McClure, 1990; Babcock, 2005).
- Avoiding conflict can result in a less-than-satisfactory tutoring relationship or in a tutor going in a different direction than what the writer intends (Seckendorf, 1986).

Taking Charge

- Taking charge entails controlling the session and attendant active and passive roles.
- Tutors can follow their own agendas if they ask closed-ended questions and drive the tutee toward a predetermined goal (Fletcher, 1993).
- The more passively tutees behaved, the more directive untrained tutors became (McClure, 1990).
- Native speaking tutors used less negotiation with NNS tutees (Thonus, 2004).
- Letting the tutee drive the session may be more empowering for the tutee, but allowing the tutor to control the session is more efficient (unless the tutor is wrong) (Seckendorf, 1986).

Active/Passive

- These roles are sometimes linked to taking charge. The active participant is the one who takes charge.
- Again, passivity in the tutee brings out directiveness in the tutor (Bell, 1989b).
- Tutees can learn to use passivity to manipulate tutors into doing more work (Jordan, 2003).
- Assertiveness can be a positive type of aggression that establishes the needs of the tutee and ensures that they are addressed (McInerney, 1998).

(Non-)authoritarian

- Tutors can use the authority of the academic institution to enhance their own position when using authority as a justification for explaining how "we" use sources in academia, for example (Murphy, 2001).
- Authority can validate praise or reinforce negativity that can hurt a tutee's feelings (Cardenas, 2000).
- Tutors can manage authority effectively by ensuring that tutees share a feeling of authority in the session (Bell, 1989b).

"Gendered" Approach

- Tutors have attempted to take feminist stances to tutoring but conflicted with tutees over feminist interpretations of their writing (Woolbright, 1992; Seckendorf, 1986).
- Tutors can be seen in a "mother" role by tutees (Callaway, 1993).
- A feminine gender role is related to an "ethic of care" that is nurturing, non-directive and non-confrontational. A masculine style would be direct and authoritative. Both happen in the writing center (Nicolas, 2002).
- Tutoring is coded as primarily feminine (Nicolas, 2002).

Power

- Tutors exercise power by asking questions and controlling the topics and types of questions; even by encouraging tutees to take charge, tutors are exercising power (Jordan, 2003).
- Tutees have the ultimate power over their text (Jordan, 2003).
- Power can change hands throughout the session (Vallejo, 2004).

Resistance

- Tutees can resist the tutor's influence and ignore any suggestions (Seckendorf, 1986; Rodby, 2002; Waring, 2005).
- Resistance occurs when tutors and tutees are at odds over what they want to accomplish and when they disagree (Seckendorf, 1986).

Teacher/Peer

- Tutors must work to cultivate the role of peer (Roswell, 1992; Bell, 1989b).
- The role of "writer" can be taken on by a tutee and implies a more peer-like relationship in that time and experience are the only differences between the tutor and tutee (Roswell, 1992).
- With NNS students, the tutor can also fill the role of "linguistic informant" (Blau, Hall, Davis & Gravitz, 2001).

- Whether or not tutors take on teacher roles is partly determined by whether or not they are teachers or meet the needs of tutees directively when asked to do so (Ritter, 2002; Seckendorf, 1986).
- Time is also a factor. Tutors are more likely to act like teachers in short-term tutoring relationships and more like peers in long-term ones (Briggs, 1991).

(In)sincerity

- Non-directivity can lead tutors to be dishonest and not foster true rapport through their actions because they hold back their opinions and are being dishonest (Statchera, 2003).

CHAPTER SIX

Emotion

Emotions play an important part in the tutoring session. Tutors and tutees can relate through emotions. A theme running through several of the sources we analyzed was that the writing center and the tutoring relationship can create communities of people who are joined in not only academic, but human, relationships. In McInerney's *A Portrait of One Writing Center through Undergraduate Tutors' Talk: Themes of Home, Heart and Head* (1998), caring and humanness differentiate the writing center from other places on campus. Tutees said of the writing center that "They treat you like a human being" and "It's like they like you there" (p.192). In the writing center emotions are allowed to be displayed through the discourse and interaction between the tutor and tutee. It is not merely a matter of the tutee turning in a paper to be graded, but a process that can run a gamut of feelings for both the tutor and tutee.

Frustration

Frustration can be a factor in the tutoring relationship. The tutor and tutee can become frustrated with the way the session is going, but also with each other, or themselves. Callaway (1993) included in her work an anecdote about Johanna, the tutor, and Kit, the tutee. In this example, Johanna was frustrated by Kit. Johanna said Kit "had no idea what to write" (p. 88). Because of Kit's low skills, Johanna, the tutor, became frustrated. This frustration led to Johanna going against her training and beliefs in tutoring to try to help the tutee. Tutors in the research studies we reviewed were also frustrated by tutees' unrealistic expectations. Tutees wanted a fix-it-shop approach, and tutors did not appreciate that (Wolcott, 1989). In the attempt to make the tutee comfortable during the session, tutors may have to go against their tutoring philosophy or training. Stachera (2003) noticed that when non-directive strategies did not work, the consultants tended to take over the session and tell the writer what to do, and this caused them to feel "any number of emotions ranging from frustration to self-doubt" (p. 218). Both tutor and tutee can have feelings of frustration and self-doubt, as when tutors go against their training, or when tutees question their own ability to write.

Sometimes tutors were frustrated by the absence of tutee feedback in online tutorials (Robertson, 2005). Tutors in Stachera's (2003) study were frustrated that tutees didn't take a more active part in sessions. They wanted tutees to talk more than they did. In one case, a tutee actually raised her hand to speak while the tutor was talking; the tutor did not see her. Blau, Hall and Strauss (1998) discussed tutors' questions and qualifiers as being frustrating to tutees. Jordan (2003) discussed a tutor who felt frustrated because she wanted to tell the writer what to do but did not because of perceived constraints on her tutoring role. Haas (1986) found that a tutor thought "the most difficult, frustrating thing about being a tutor is you feel you have to teach logic and ideas and it's really very difficult. That's why grammar and structure are easier to deal with" (p. 151).

McInerney (1998) observed a tutee's frustration through body language: "Folding her arms and squirming around" gave the observer the impression that "she was uneasy and didn't know how to fix her paper" (p. 158). In one case in Cardenas (2000), a tutor and tutee were both frustrated when collaboration did not occur. In this case, the tutor attempted to get the student to collaborate, but since the student acted as a "recipient of information" (p. 83), probably because of his "difficulties in writing the document" and lack of knowledge, "the interaction reinforce[d] the perception that [the tutee] ha[d] a lack of writing proficiency" (p. 87). In this case, the tutor ended up being more directive than he would have liked.

Cardenas found that unsuccessful attempts at collaboration often resulted in frustration. For instance, in Carter-Tod (1995), a NNS tutee came for specific directive feedback and instead got reassurance and questions about how she approached the assignment and what she wanted to say. This resulted in frustration for the tutee. Lerner (1996) also found tutors frustrated with NNS tutorials due to the "tension between tutor and student goals" (p. 251).

Fear

Fear is not just an emotion for tutees who feel they will be stigmatized by seeking counsel from the writing center. Fear can also be felt by tutors who work at the center. McInerney (1998) included the following anecdote from one of her tutors, which she then analyzed. The tutor, Kristen, is speaking:

> "My closest friends, when told of my desire to tutor in the Center, cringed. They exploded in curses about the Center and shared their fears about entering 'that' room. They admitted that the tutors they knew were kind and relatively fun people. Nonetheless, the physical room and the 'idea of' the Center to them, was overwhelmingly scary and intimidating. I quickly assured them that it was not a scary place and that they should feel comfortable there. I was, of course, being hypocritical, for I too shared those views." Already, Kristin assumes the role of ambassador for the Center, attempting to disabuse students of their fear of the Center and replace that with ideas of "comfortable." (p. 116)

Tutors can also become stigmatized from working in the writing center. However, in terms of emotions, they do not seek to continue this stigmatization; rather, they seek to destroy the negative and enhance the positive, even when they do not necessarily feel that way.

Apprehension is related to fear, as in another case McInerney presented in which the tutee felt that her work just wasn't good enough. In this case, the tutee repeatedly described her paper as "sucky" (p. 140), and the tutor, in turn, explained that these problems were "typical to rough drafts, and not insurmountable." Another tutor in McInerney's study was extremely worried about her writing, so she chose to see a tutor with less experience but with whom she had a good relationship. Severino (1992) reported a tutee feeling apprehension about his teacher and "his faithfulness to the interviewee and her story" (p. 59). The medium of online tutoring also contributed to tutors' fear, especially if they were not comfortable with the technology (Robertson, 2005).

Fear can also manifest itself in discouragement. Magnotto (1991) discussed a tutee in one of the conferences she observed who was extremely discouraged about her paper. She did not think the teacher was going to like her paper, and she was also concerned that the teacher was not going to grade the paper fairly: "I really don't want to do the paper because I feel as though she's not going to grade it right. She's not even going to finish reading my paper if it doesn't sound right to her" (p. 190). Her tutor in turn encouraged her by reminding her that this was just a beginning, and then later that it was just a rough draft.

Guilt

Guilt, throughout this research, seemed primarily to be felt by the tutors, probably because of their training in non-directive tutoring styles. Blau, Hall and Sparks (2002) in "Guilt-Free Tutoring: Rethinking How We Tutor Non-Native-English-Speaking Students" sought to address the feeling of guilt caused by tutors practicing techniques that went against their training. Blau, Hall and Sparks declared that in tutorials with non-native speakers it was necessary for the tutor to go against training for the tutoring session to be effective. The authors suggested revising tutor training to achieve guilt-free tutoring. Directivity caused guilt in a tutoring relationship that Callaway (1993) studied. When the tutor directed the tutee on how to improve her paper, she felt guilty; however, this process pleased the tutee and resulted in a productive session. Haas (1986) described a tutoring dyad in which both tutor and tutee felt guilt, the tutor because "she had not succeeded in helping Evelyn learn correctness," and the tutee, Evelyn, because "she cannot get it right" (p. 150).

Confusion

Tutors in Jordan's (2003) study saw confusion as a positive factor in the tutoring sessions, as confusion caused students to ask questions, resulting in the tutor's realization that they may have told the tutee the wrong thing. In one conference that Bell (1989b) observed, a tutee was upset and confused at the end of a conference. The tutee was comfortable with the tutor, but was trying to argue a position in her paper that she did not actually hold. Bell and Youmans (2006) noted that non-native English speaking tutees became confused when tutors used a politeness strategy that included praising the paper, when indeed the paper needed a lot of work. In a study by Woolbright (1992) the tutee became confused due to the mismatch between the feminist reading the tutor was attempting to formulate and the patriarchal, dominant discourse of thesis support.

Comfort

Our grounded theory analysis found that comfort can mean the tutor and tutee feeling comfortable with each other, the tutee feeling more comfortable with the process of writing, or the tutor feeling comfortable with talking about writing. In one case, McClure (1990) observed a tutor who was uncomfortable with the student's paper topic, which caused a mismatch in what the writer wanted and what the tutor did. Bean (1998) wrote about a tutor who felt comfortable with the nurturing approach to tutoring advocated by her director, and that she valued "her ability to make connections with students and help them become more confident with themselves as writers" (p. 140). Hunter (1993) wrote about comfort and confidence in the writer resulting from "talk-off-task" events which are "pleasant, human exchanges" (pp. 207–208). Ritter (2002) observed NS tutors being uncomfortable tutoring NNS tutees, sometimes to the point of taking over sessions and making corrections that changed the meaning to other than what the writer intended. One tutor in McInerney's (1998) study felt it was important for her to make the student feel comfortable. Some writers, such as McClure (1990), described this process as putting the tutee "at ease." Cardenas (2000) also noted that in successful collaborations, tutees felt "at ease" (p. 112).

McInerney acknowledged that not all tutees are looking for a close connection, and to "create comfort, tutors need to respect that not all students want to or have experience with engaging effectively with learning, share the passion that the tutors have for learning, or want to be in the 'family' of the center" (p. 165). Stachera (2003) found that tutors were extremely comfortable talking about writing, which sometimes led to them talking more in the session, or feeling more comfortable reading the paper aloud, even if the student expressed a desire to read, perhaps related to comfort in being in control of the session. One of the tutors in Stachera's study (2003) modified her dress to "make the students feel more comfortable" (p. 184). The tutor chose to wear jeans rather than a suit. Eckard (2001) observed that students were more comfortable in the writing center and one-on-one conferencing environment than the classroom. Because of this comfort they were more likely to talk and share stories. Tutors in Roswell's (1992) study felt they were not peers to the tutees they worked with, and thus they worked hard "to put the student at ease," to "strive to create a conversational atmosphere," and to cultivate "an informal dialogue with the tutee" (pp. 112–113), all to increase the tutee's comfort in the tutoring session.

Jordan (2003) explained that a tutee's comfort level was important, so she could jump "in with comments and questions. However, not all tutees have such a high comfort level; therefore, in a similar situation, many tutees might remain silent, perhaps never working through an application of the concept" (p. 144). Comfort can also be taken a step too far, as Melnick (1984) described. She noted that although the tutor and the tutee should strive for membership or forming a relationship with each other, if it is carried too far they will actually lose the focus of the conference and cause it to become a personal conversation.

Summary

- Tutors and tutees relate through emotion.
- Emotions allow for the creation of communities and belonging (McInerney, 1998).

Frustration

- Tutors and clients can become frustrated if their expectations are thwarted (Wolcott, 1989; Carter-Tod, 1995; Lerner, 1996).
- Tutors become frustrated when a client's needs force the tutor into strategies they do not feel comfortable using (Stachera, 2003; Callaway, 1993).

- Tutors can also become frustrated when tutees are non-responsive, and both tutor and client can be frustrated when collaboration fails to materialize; however, frustration is exacerbated when either tries to force collaboration (Stachera, 2003; Cardenas, 2000).

Fear

- The writing center itself can elicit fear in potential clients, even potential tutors, in large part because of the intellectual power it holds in the minds of many (McInerney, 1998).
- Some tutees feel their work is inadequate and feel anxious about revealing it to the tutor; others feel apprehension about meeting teacher expectations (McInerney, 1998; Magnotto, 1991).
- Online tutorials can also create a sense of fear in those who are not at ease with computer technology (Robertson, 2005).

Guilt

- If there is a sense of guilt, it is most often felt by a tutor who feels forced to abandon the student-centered, non-directive techniques in favor of a more directive approach to a tutorial (Blau, Hall & Sparks, 2002; Callaway, 1993).
- Guilt can be felt by both tutor and tutee when they feel they have failed to meet each other's goals (Haas, 1986).

Confusion

- Tutors frequently view confusion as a good thing because it usually spawns helpful questions and interactions from the clients (Jordan, 2003).
- Non-native speakers can be confused by the politeness strategies tutors employ (Bell & Youmans, 2006).
- Confusion can arise from tutors and tutees discussing views or concepts that they do not hold or that do not apply to the work at hand (Bell, 1989b; Wolcott, 1992).

Comfort

- Comfort is manifested in several ways: the tutor and tutee becoming comfortable with one another; a tutee becoming comfortable with writing as a process; a tutor becoming comfortable about talking about writing.
- Discomfort can arise when a client's topic or work is antithetical to the tutor's views (McClure, 1990).
- Comfort is often developed with casual, off-topic chats (Hunter, 1993).
- Discomfort sometimes arose between tutors and non-native speakers (Ritter, 2002).
- Tutors actively strove to put clients at ease, especially those who felt they were not genuine peers to those they tutored. One tutor even consciously chose casual attire to make the clients more comfortable (Roswell, 1992; McInerney, 1998; McClure, 1990; Stachera, 2003).
- Some tutors become so comfortable in their positions that they can create less than optimum tutorials as they take control of the session to the detriment of the client (Stachera, 2003).
- Tutees seem more comfortable in the writing center atmosphere than in the classroom, which creates greater opportunities for story-telling (Eckard, 2001).
- Lack of comfort on the part of a tutee may result in issues being ignored because of the tutee's reticence (Jordan, 2003).
- Conversely, comfort can be counter-productive if the level of comfort is such that the session loses its focus on writing (Melnick, 1984).

CHAPTER SEVEN

Temperament

The temperament of each individual involved in the session is an important factor. Although temperament can be seen as a person's natural state, something stable, it can also be slipped in and out of as the situation dictates. The traditional aspects of temperament are the humors, or sanguine, melancholic, choleric, and phlegmatic. Instead of amusing ourselves with these categories, we have adopted those that arose from the data. These are (in)sensitivity, confidence and empathy.

(In)sensitivity

According to McInerney (1998), sensitivity deals with issues "such as reading signals, understanding body language, and reading between the lines" (p.127) A tutor in McInerney's study explained that "in order to establish a [tutorial] relationship, you must be able to catch the subtle hints a student gives or be ready to incorporate those things the student brings with him or her..." (pp. 159–160). Sensitivity is also related to McInerney's concept of "openness" in which "the tutor attempts to structure the environment of the session so that he or she has permission to understand the student..." (p. 157).

Cardenas (2000) mentioned two instances in which the tutor was not sensitive to the tutee's needs which led to an ineffective session. It seems as if sensitivity is closely tied to responsiveness. For a person to respond to another's cues, they first must be sensitive to their existence. In one session, the tutor was not sensitive to what the tutee wanted from the conference and went off on her own topic, not aware of messages the tutee was sending about what she wanted out of the conversation. The student had wanted to work on brainstorming, but the tutor insisted on working on organization. The tutee even expressed this fact several times, but the tutor did not pick up on it, and pressed on with her ideas for the session. Hunter (1993) noticed that sometimes the tutor was not responsive to the tutee's needs, creating conflict or apathy in the tutoring session:

> [Yvonne, the tutee] did not understand what Paula [the tutor] was trying to explain to her, and she did not understand its importance. She was therefore beginning to lose patience and to suspect that Paula wasn't a very good tutor. At this point in the conference, Yvonne's attitude seemed to shift. From here through the end of the session, she appeared to be merely enduring Paula. (p. 129)

Hunter reported that Yvonne would not work with the tutors again if she felt she must endure their questions in order to get their help. Basically, as long as Yvonne was happy she was willing to work with the tutor, but if a negative attitude change took place in Yvonne while working with the tutor, she would not work with that tutor again.

Thonus (1999b) found tutors working with NNS tutees were very sensitive to their understanding of Speech Acts and used Illocutionary Force Indicating Devices (IFID). For example, a tutor would give an indirect suggestion and then say, "That's just a suggestion," or, before giving a recommendation, a tutor said, "I have to recommend that you do it this way" (p. 274). This helped the non-native speakers, as otherwise they may have misunderstood the tutor's intent.

Jordan (2003) discussed responsiveness as the willingness of the other participant in the conference to take up the topics introduced by the interlocutor. The possibility also exists for the other party to change or ignore the introduced topic. Another form of responsiveness noted by Jordan was the willingness of conference participants to offer up needed information. Responsiveness can also be linked to indirectness—as when a tutee is obviously not picking up on a tutor's hint—the tutor can either drop it, keep at it, perhaps further confusing the tutee, or just come out and say what she means. Nicolas (2002) observed a male tutor working with a female tutee, and in the tutoring session the tutee told the tutor that her friend had just died (pg. 173). Instead of engaging with the important topic of her friends' death, the tutor asked her about a grammatical point. This illustrates what we've noticed about grammar being a fall back and possibly a marker of male and female tutoring styles. In DiPardo (1992) the tutor, Morgan, seemed insensitive to the tutee's needs related to her background and identity. DiPardo also implied that if Morgan had gotten to know her tutee better, she would have realized that Fannie was an ESL student and an outsider to academic culture.

Confidence

Confidence is needed by both the tutor and tutee. A tutee can influence a tutor's confidence as seen in Callaway (1993). When reflecting on her tutoring of Kit, Johanna felt Kit "was intimidated by the breadth of her difficulties with written communication, and I think I manifested my subsequent feelings of anxiety with rigidity and a conservative approach to tutoring" (p. 92). Johanna's feelings and reactions to her tutee affected her confidence.

Confidence is also important to the tutee, and tutors use different tools to inspire confidence in the tutee's writing abilities. Bell (1989b) had two separate tutors remark on how confidence needed to be inspired in the tutees. One tutor told Bell that her tutee "needed encouragement" and that "at the pre-writing stage...it is a matter of reinforcing her self-confidence and helping her develop initiative to go ahead with her project" (pp. 77–78). One of the tutors in Robertson's (2005) study of online tutoring thought that confidence was built face-to-face, rather than online. An L2 tutee in one of Carter-Tod's case studies (1995) lacked confidence in her writing, although her tutors thought her writing was quite good. One of the tutors in Jordan's (2003) study implied that tutees come to the writing center *because* they lack confidence; hence, they want feedback on their writing. She suggested that writing center tutors could give them confidence that "their ideas are important and that they can achieve something without someone deciding everything for them" (p. 106).

Jordan coded confidence as a factor in empowerment, the focus of her study. She concluded that "increased confidence reflects empowerment" (p. 117). Tutors in Jordan's (2003) study noted that they could use their authority and power to affirm insecure students that they are "okay" (p. 105), thus empowering them. Bell (1989b) noted that tutees' lack of confidence may have resulted in a lack of assertiveness in the tutoring session, while the reverse could also be true. A highly confident person is more likely to assert his or her desires for the direction the conference takes. Bell also noted that sometimes tutors enhance tutee's confidence through praise (see section on Praise).

Empathy

The natural disposition for most tutors is to empathize with a tutee to establish rapport, such as sharing personal stories to make the tutee comfortable in the session. Eckard (2001) noted tutors empathizing with tutees by using comments such as "I understand," and "I feel that way about writing sometimes" (p. 65). One of the tutors in Stachera's (2003) study cultivated empathy as a tutoring skill:

> I think we have to be empathetic with them
> we have to be empathetic
> we have to be professional
> we have to know what we are doing
> we have to know how to do it
> but we have to be empathetic
> we have to be able to feel what they are feeling to a certain extent. (p. 184, ethnopoetic notation original)

Empathy is also related to encouragement, as McInerney (1998) noted in her study. Women, as observed in Hunzer (1997), are sometimes stereotyped as being more empathetic than men.

Summary

Temperament

- In our analysis, we determined that while temperament is a natural state, people can adjust and adapt it, so it is malleable even if generally stable.

(In)sensitivity

- Sensitivity deals with a person's ability to "read" the subtle signals sent by others through body language and other verbal and non-verbal signals (McInerney, 1998).
- Sensitivity also can be seen as "openness" or willingness to adapt to another's needs: In this case, the needs or preferences of a client (McInerney, 1998).
- Sensitivity is tied to responsiveness, and a failure of sensitivity can lead to ineffective or even failed tutorials when the tutee felt frustrated or apathetic as a result of the tutor's behavior (Cardenas, 2000; Hunter, 1993).
- Non-native speakers were benefitted by tutors who used Illocutionary Force Indicating Devices to explain the meaning of their comments (Thonus, 1999b).
- Responsiveness, an aspect of sensitivity, contains the potential for reciprocity between both parties, such as to provide information, the willingness to ignore an issue (indirectness), or to move past an issue with a more direct approach (Jordan, 2003).
- Insensitivity can lead to the fall-back position of tutoring grammar when a client presents information beyond the parameters of a typical tutorial (Nicolas, 2002), or when the client's background and experience are not taken into account (DiPardo, 1992).

Confidence

- Confidence is important to both the tutor and the tutee, and tutors use a variety of techniques to inspire confidence in their clients (Callaway, 1993; Bell, 1989b).
- Some tutors believe confidence cannot be inspired in an online environment (Robertson 2005).
- Sometimes confidence is not related to writing ability (Carter-Tod, 1995).
- Confidence is an empowering factor, and tutors can use their authority to affirm and thus inspire self-confidence in their tutees (Jordan, 2003).

- Lack of confidence in tutees can lead to passivity in a conference, while the reverse can also be true, and praise can help inspire confidence (Bell, 1989b).

Empathy

- Tutors strive to employ empathy through language and actively use it as a tutoring skill (Eckard, 2001; Stachera 2003).
- Empathy is associated with encouragement (McInerney, 1998), and it is a stereotypically female trait (Hunzer, 1997).

CHAPTER EIGHT

Outcome

When all the factors discussed in the previous chapters converge, they create the focus of the tutoring session, which results in the outcome. The focus of the session is usually some aspect of the writer's text or writing process in general. The outcome of the session can be affective, such as an improved attitude toward writing; cognitive, such as enhanced knowledge about writing processes; or material, such as an improved paper. Some outcomes can happen during or after the session. For example, trust can be established during the session, or it may take several sessions to establish (Callaway, 1993). Comfort and trust are both outcomes of the session. A tutor seeks to inspire positive emotions while dispelling the negative to create a comfortable atmosphere which will allow the tutee to learn and make the session more amiable to collaboration. Cardenas (2000) wrote about the many emotional and affective sources of a successful outcome: "Growth in writing behaviors relates to the secure emotional well-being that [the tutee] experienced. The ease that she feels may result from the deference shown to her as the authority and relaxed, conversational tone" (pp. 112–113).

Session Focus

The session focus depends on the negotiation of concerns between the tutor and tutee. Sometimes an ESL student will come to the tutoring session wanting to focus on grammar, but the tutor will see more pressing issues in the paper having to do with logic or idea development (Blau, Hall, & Sparks, 2002). Bean (1999) found that sometimes the session focus depended on the perception of the tutors, which she claimed was based on gender. She interviewed two tutors, Julie and Daniel. Julie thought that tutors attended to grammar and mechanics when they were in a hurry and wanted to "move the session along quickly" (p. 135), while Daniel saw attention to grammar and line-by-line analysis as attending to the concerns of the tutee. Roswell (1992) observed little introductory talk and agenda setting, and very few sessions were student-centered. Most she observed were text-centered, but the text was "not just an artifact present in the setting, but [was] a voice in the conversation, in many cases, in fact, the primary voice and the one to which both the student and tutor respond" (p. 183). Sometimes what the tutors found extremely interesting and important, for example, diction in Wolcott (1989), was "a source of disinterest to most students" (p. 23). Sometimes the session focus was contested between the desires of the tutor, tutee and teacher (Haas, 1986).

Student-centered. Truly student-centered conferences were rare in the data. But student-centered is not synonymous with non-directive. Vallejo (2004) found that tutors often asked NNS tutees what they wanted to work on, and more often that not, this was grammar. The tutors took a fairly directive approach and the students made minimal responses. "When the tutoring sessions shifted to global issues of writing, a nondirective tutoring stance was then used" (p. 71). Cardenas (2000) noted only three truly student-centered conferences out of thirty she observed. In the student-centered conferences the tutors deferred to the tutees as experts, and the tutees were assertive in what they wanted to accomplish in the tutorial. Cardenas categorized the student-centered conferences as examples of "minimalist tutoring."

Tutor-centered. Sometimes tutors had an "ideal" text in mind and this cast them in the "contradictory role of 'hunched-shouldered authority' and demanded of student writers an equally paradoxical stance of 'active compliance'" (Roswell, 1992, pp. v–vi). The tutors in Stachera's (2003) study were extremely comfortable talking about writing, to the extent that they talked more and sometimes didn't notice that the tutee wanted to participate. In fact, Stachera observed a tutee raising her hand when she had something to say, but the tutor was so busy talking he didn't see her. Bell (1989b) wrote of a tutor who was aware that he "ran the conference" but that he "seemed quite happy to let [the tutee] take the initiative, and he was careful about his role as an authority" (p. 158).

Bell mentioned another tutor in his study who took over the session and was very direct: This so disarmed the tutee that she ceased participating in the session. The tutor actually may have lowered the tutee's confidence. However, in one tutor-centered conference in particular that Bell observed, although the tutor steered the direction of the conference, at no time did he attempt to interfere with the content and substance of the writer's paper. Wolcott (1989) found that most of the conferences she studied were teacher-centered, probably because the tutors were older graduate students. In Vallejo's (2004) study, the topic of grammar resulted in a tutor-centered conference. One of the tutors in Lerner's (1996) study found that she became more directive once a relationship had been established.

Text-centered. Roswell (1992) observed very few student-centered conferences. Most were text-centered, in which "the text is objectified, the text's integrity is acknowledged, and the text is the occasion of all response" (pp. 182–183). The text-centered conference usually focused on grammar, and there are various reasons why this might occur. Nicolas (2002) observed that tutoring sessions fell back on grammar as a neutral default territory when participants could not make a connection. On the other hand, Bell (1989b) observed a tutoring session between two women who were relaxed and friendly with each other and whose session focused mostly on editing for style. The participants were pleased with the session and the tutor said it was "fun" (p. 105). Magnotto (1991) also observed an extremely confident, strong writer work on grammar.

Sometimes the tutee wanted a text-centered conference and the tutor resisted this because of training. In a dyad Callaway (1993) described, the tutee wanted to talk about her text while the tutor wanted to talk about writing in general. In their sixth session of the semester, the tutor felt the conference was a failure because she commented on the student's draft and gave her suggestions for improvement. However, the student was pleased to receive directive comments on her draft and was very happy with the session. In some of the tutorials McLure (1990) studied, the conference became so text-centered that the consultant became more "engrossed in the draft," while the tutee "signaled growing inattention as well as dissatisfaction" with body language, such as pushing the chair away from the table (p. 155). Bean (1998) found that the topic of grammar itself tended to "create rigid roles, with the consultant in the position of authority and the student in a position of ignorance" (p. 149). However, she did describe a conference based on grammar that showed reciprocity and balance. Online tutorials are entirely text-based (Robertson, 2005).

Authority

Roswell (1992) found that "the length of time a dyad worked together and degree of solidarity between tutor and writer were extremely important factors in the attribution of authority" (p. 182). Ritter (2002) noted that authority was related to comfort in the tutoring session—that tutors who perceived they had less authority were not comfortable working with ESL students and tended to work on "grammar rather than writing because they were not comfortable with the type of research papers the students had…it is not a simple action for some tutors to focus on writing before grammar" (p. 283), while Bean (1998) found that male tutors struggled against the role of authority. Vallejo (2004) found that NNS tutees desired tutors to have more authority and preferred directive tutoring. They were dissatisfied when the tutor suggested they do outside research when they believed the tutor had the answer and was holding it back. Authority could be thrust upon the tutor by the other participant in the tutoring session. Seckendorf (1986) found that the tutor, Joan, actually used her authority to verbally "beat up" a student by trying to convince her that her paper was about what Joan thought, not what the tutee thought it was about. Melnick (1984) found that tutors could balance their authority by remaining aware of the speech dynamic between themselves and the tutee as it was transpiring, while McClure (1990) noticed that the tutor with the "least authority" would work on just what the tutee wanted to work on and not attempt to push her own agenda. Another tutor in the study, Ann, had more authority and would use it to give praise and advice.

Material Outcomes

Sometimes the outcome of the session was material as manifested in an improved paper or improved writing ability in the student. Williams (2004) found that the improvement in a writer might not be externally measurable. The writer may have gained skills and attitudes, but these were not necessarily apparent in the students' written work. Haas (1986) described a tutoring session in which a tutee was able to totally reconceive her text based on the tutor's praise and her resulting comfort. Wolcott (1989) wrote that writing skill and improved attitude about writing were outcomes of the session. Carter-Tod (1995) traced the revisions the L2 tutees in her study made after their writing center visits, which ranged from editing for idiomatic English to deep rhetorical and structural changes. One tutor in her study measured the success of a tutoring session "in terms of how many 'problems' were 'solved'" (p. 129).

Relationship

During the course of the tutoring session, or over several sessions, the tutor and tutee develop a relationship. This relationship is characterized by solidarity, trust and comfort (or the lack thereof), and is displayed in the tutoring session through collaboration and conflict, authority, and empowerment. Melnick (1984) described the process of relationship building through the concept of membershipping—"the process by which speakers share varying degrees of intellectual and social belonging in a conversation" (p. 10). Sometimes this process could enhance the comfort of the tutee, but sometimes it could go too far, resulting in a personal conversation rather than a tutoring session. Haas (1986) noted the importance of rapport in the tutoring session. She gave examples of playfulness, laughter and interruptions as evidence of rapport and relationship-building. McInerney (1998) found the relationship to be the most important part of the tutoring interaction. She wrote of the "bond with others that fosters learning" (p. 186) and that the writing center is a place for "human interaction and dialogue" (p. 187).

Solidarity. Connectedness, rapport and chemistry are what lead to solidarity. A connection must be felt for a union to stand strong; however, if there is no rapport or chemistry, it is merely a feeling of connection, but not an actual union—therefore there cannot truly be solidarity (something will be able to divide it). Chemistry would fall under an intuition, an automatic "clicking" of two personalities which fosters a feeling of connectedness which can lead to solidarity. Rapport is a method of interaction for the personalities involved. There can be good and bad rapport, and they contribute to the work of the session once they are established. Female tutors in Bean's (1998) study downplayed their authority in order to create more solidarity with tutees. Tutors in Carter-Tod's (1995) study reported that "mutual understanding" between them and the tutees was essential for a successful tutoring session (p. 129).

Solidarity between tutor and tutee stems from a positive relationship. A positive relationship grows from positive rapport. It is not necessary to establish positive rapport or even solidarity for a tutorial session to be effective (see previous section on [dis]honesty). It is, however, beneficial. Solidarity is based on a unified sense of purpose and mutual respect rather than, say, affection. For instance, in the session reported in Bell's 1990 work that described a tutee who felt disarmed by her highly directive tutor, lack of solidarity accounted for the tutee's alienation, just as it accounted for the feelings of guilt some tutors felt when they were forced from their traditional, non-directive approach into more directive approaches. Thus, solidarity is closely tied to focus and role.

Trust. Trust doesn't always come easily or automatically. One tutor in Bean's study (1999) was a big man who took up a lot of space and reported that he had to work harder to get students to trust him because of his physical presence. A tutor and tutee in Callaway's (1993) study, Johanna and Cassie, had an interesting relationship, and we (the authors) are not entirely sure that Callaway fully captured it or understood it. Cassie and Johanna's relationship was conflicted at first, but in the end they built trust and were able to have a productive tutoring session. At first,

Cassie was resistant. Then Johanna was frustrated because she did not want to take over the text as that went against her training and philosophy. In the end, however, she changed her approach and gave direct feedback. The tutee still resisted the feedback. But then she had a change of attitude and was satisfied with the tutoring session. Johanna and the researcher (Callaway) discussed whether Cassie's resistance might have had to do with Johanna as an audience and how Cassie might have felt vulnerable. There was also an issue about them both being writers, but Cassie was admitted to the university provisionally, so she didn't have that stamp of approval on her writing. Cassie and Johanna may have also felt competitive, with the flip side of that being equality. Johanna said,

> I somehow present being competitive with her, and she picked up on that, or it was a good thing in that she saw me as an equal.... So, maybe she saw me as an equal in which case it would be very good because it would be more of a peer tutoring situation. (p. 459)

Cassie was also skeptical about some advice Johanna gave early on in the sessions that may not have been correct. In addition, Cassie had a lot of resentment and may have reflected that onto her tutor as a representative of the academy.

At first, Cassie was very resistant about talking about her writing. She had a lot of excuses, probably because she did not want to be vulnerable in front of her tutor. Cassie also had a lot of ambivalence about wanting/not wanting criticism of her work. The tutor felt Cassie was "a very competent writer" (p. 404) but Cassie didn't want to hear it. But when Johanna suggested some revision, Cassie was resistant and said she wanted to keep her text as it was. The change came when Johanna showed Cassie some of her own poems which built equality and trust.

Sometimes just talking wasn't enough. Callaway wrote that another factor could be that Johanna didn't take into account that Cassie was an outsider to academia, being Black. In addition, Johanna didn't have a problem mixing her creative and academic writing, but for Cassie, they were very separate. Carter-Tod (1995) described a tutoring dyad in which the relationship and trust they developed were an important factor in the tutoring sessions. When a tutor and tutee developed trust they could move from "editing, to regular visits with Ruth [the tutor] for feedback and response throughout the entire composing process" (p. 85).

Empowerment. Jordan (2003) found the outcome of the session to be empowerment—empowerment of the writer through enhanced writing skills—or critical empowerment as a person who has control over discourse and thus can control in some sense his or her world.

Happiness/satisfaction. Bell (1989b) categorized successful tutoring sessions as those from which all participants emerged happy. Cassie, the tutee in Callaway's (1993) study, was finally happy with the tutoring session in which the tutor gave her direct feedback on her paper.

Collaboration and conflict. Rodby (2002) wrote about conflict, which is probably the result of the tutor and tutee failing to connect. In a tutoring session she observed, two undergraduates were working on a paper for a recreation course; the tutee seemed at odds culturally with the very notion of recreation. The student defended his paper against the teacher's comments, all the while not understanding what the teacher wanted. The tutor attempted to explain the assignment while the tutee continued to resist. The tutor finally encouraged the student to be creative. He again resisted. The tutor then gave up and suggested they work on spelling instead (p. 226). The author said the conflict was about discourses—entering them, resisting them—and when in conflict, the student resisted entering the discourse of recreation which seemed foreign to him. Rodby suspected this was because of his status as a Mexican-American child of farm workers and grandchild of illegal immigrants; he had a different relation to leisure than the assignment assumed. Like so many other tutorials with conflict, and in this case, a concomitant lack of solidarity, this one fell back to spelling and grammar when the tutor saw that the student was not going to engage the goals of the assignment that the teacher expected.

Callaway (1993) said perhaps resistance is a crucial factor in collaboration, and resistance is necessary to result in a productive session. In the tutoring dyad she described, the tutee wanted a text-centered conference while the tutor wanted a relationship. It was not time effective, however, as the first productive tutoring session of the fall semester in the dyad she described occurred on November 30. Callaway commented,

> Collaboration occurs when the student writer is genuinely involved in a dialogic relationship with her text, her teacher, and the tutor. When Cassie entered the session on November 30 to discuss an assignment, she was embroiled in a conversation with her text that she had not experienced up to that point. And Johanna, by taking a more conflicted role, deepened her conversation. The dialogism of a student writer like Cassie may involve contention or resistance to the assignment, to the academy as a whole, or even to the tutor; in fact, in this case conflict was a prerequisite for collaboration to take place. (pp. 191–192)

Callaway noted that unsuccessful attempts at collaboration often resulted in frustration for both the tutor and tutee. Successful collaborations, on the other hand, resulted from "personal interaction...secure emotional well-being...deference...relaxed, conversational tone...[and] friendly, interactive environment" (pp. 112–13).

Severino described a collaborative conference as one in which "participants put aside the local issues of text...physically they stop looking at the student's paper, put down their pens, and start looking at each other and conversing about global, rhetorical issues" (1992, p. 62). She implied that global concerns were more likely to result in collaboration than local ones, but Bell's research (1989b) implied still different results, as a pair worked on writing style in a successful, collaborative session. Cardenas (2000) noted that successful tutoring sessions were not necessarily collaborative. Sometimes the student chose to defer to the tutor's authority, possibly because the tutors in her study were graduate students and teachers, but this could also be seen in Thonus' studies of NNS students who wanted and needed a directive approach. Boudreaux (1998) defined collaboration as "honest questions and real exchange of ideas" (p. 17).

Seckendorf (1986) found that the tutoring relationship became more collaborative over time, as the tutor and tutee figured themselves out and settled into their roles. This happened over several tutoring sessions, as one session did not seem to be enough for two people to adjust to each other's styles. In contrast, the other dyad that Seckendorf studied never adjusted, even over several tutoring sessions. This seemed to stem from the tutor's desire to avoid conflict. Because they never confronted the conflicts they felt, they were not able to get over them and into a collaborative relationship, and in fact, their conflict actually escalated to the point that they openly disagreed over the tutee's interpretations in her paper. Jordan (2003) found that collaboration and hierarchy were on a continuum and could not be discretely separated.

Summary

Outcome

- Outcomes result from the combined effects of all the elements discussed in the foregoing chapters and range from such affective elements such as trust or comfort to changed attitudes.

Session Focus

- Session focus may be student-centered, text-centered or tutor-centered.
- The session focus often needed to be negotiated with NNS tutees (Blau, Hall & Sparks, 2002; Vallejo, 2004).
- A focus on grammar can be seen as student-centered (Bean, 1999; Vallejo, 2004), tutor-centered (Vallejo, 2004) or text-centered (Bell, 1989b; Magnotto, 1991; Bean, 1998).
- The text can itself generate the session focus (Roswell, 1992), especially in on-line sessions, which are entirely text-based (Robertson, 2005).
- Tutors and tutees may not agree on what is interesting (Wolcott 1989), and the focus may be disputed between tutor, tutee and instructor (Haas, 1986).

Authority

- Authority was sometimes determined by the length of the tutorial relationship (Roswell, 1992).
- Tutors struggled with the amount of authority they had and tried to balance it with tutee's desires (Bean, 1999; Vallejo, 2004; Melnick, 1984).
- Tutors sometimes misused their authority (Seckendorf, 1986).
- Tutors with the least authority tended to adhere to the tutee's agenda (McClure, 1990) and were less comfortable (Ritter, 2002).

Material Outcomes

- Material outcomes are often not externally measureable (Williams 2004), such as improved skills (Wolcott, 1989; Carter-Tod, 1995), attitudes or even project focus (Haas, 1986).

Relationship

- The tutor/tutee relationship is characterized by solidarity, trust, and comfort or the lack thereof. Melnick (1984) called this membershipping and found that it can be positive or negative to the outcome.
- Rapport is important according to Haas (1986).
- McInerney (1998) found that relationship was the most important determining element to the tutorial outcome.
- Important features of the relationship include solidarity, trust, empowerment, happiness/satisfaction and collaboration and conflict.

CHAPTER NINE

Conclusion

As we established at the outset, we sought to use grounded theory analysis to develop a theory or framework for writing center tutoring. We concluded that the theory, framework, or process by which tutors and tutees encounter one another forms a context composed of personal characteristics and outside influences with the result of creating the session focus, the energy of which is generated through a continuum of collaboration and conflict. Since the temperament and emotions of the tutor and tutee interplay with the other factors in the session, such as the roles each chooses to take on, the form that the session focus ultimately takes is dynamic. Whatever form the session focus appears in, or whatever it is designed to address, the sum of all the session's and participants' influences produce the outcome of the session. The outcome may be affective, cognitive, material, or a combination of these traits.

What has yet to be determined, however, are the participants' levels of satisfaction and the work they actually achieve; we shall deal with this concept when we discuss definitions of success. We must also consider the goals of the faculty and the limitations universities place on Writing Centers these outside influences, in our opinion, have been under-discussed. We hope this study will serve as a description and not a prescription for creating session foci that meet the needs of tutors, tutees, and the faculty, and is a "both and" rather than an "either/or" take on the purpose and use of Writing Centers that still does not stray from the path to the long-cherished end of creating more confident and competent writers. Creating this synthesis was an attempt to synthesize findings in Writing Center scholarship and this true synthesis became our goal as we sought to reconcile internal contradictions between and among our theoretical findings.

Relation to Other Scholarship

With the synthesis complete, we can tie in a few more published works (both studies included in the data set and others) relevant to our findings. In this section we bring in the commentary of researchers whose studies were included in the synthesis, as our research method focused on just the data presented, not researcher commentary. We can now bring in that commentary and put it in dialogue with our findings and other sources. As we began working on this book, we noticed that several of our discoveries were in line with the discoveries of others, all of which turn accepted methods of tutoring upside down or otherwise alter writing center methodologies that have long been in stasis. This not only evidences the quality of the synthesis, but demonstrates that Writing Center researchers have, for decades, been moving toward a synthesis of theory and practice. The intersections of our findings with the various bits of research we will present—material published after we completed our analysis, material we overlooked, or work that bears surprising resemblance to ours—represent the main points at which the conclusions produced in this synthesis become particularly salient. While correlation certainly does not indicate the "right" answer to a theoretical question, or a question about writing center praxis, it illustrates common concern and a common effort to stray, deliberately, outside accepted bounds.

To wit, a 1989 article by Hynds that we missed in our original analysis—most likely because it appeared in a relatively obscure journal—reinforced many of our findings. Writers in Hynds' study experienced dissonance and discomfort and were not likely to discuss these feelings or to negotiate goals or roles. And as we found with collaboration and conflict, she too saw that a dyad could either get stuck in their conflict or move through it to a more satisfactory outcome. As we found with expectations, writers in Hynds' study also made inferences about each other which were often incorrect or in conflict. Participants also demonstrated some emotions we found and some we did not, such as insecurity, intimidation, a lack of confidence, guilt and frustration. Hynds' framework is also an interesting comparison to ours. She found that the content dimension included "aspects of the text under discussion, the interpersonal behaviors of both participants, and the strategies used by the consultant." The belief dimension included "the perceptions, needs, goals, and perceived roles of both participants" (p. 80). It is almost uncanny how closely our categories and analyses reflect Hynds'.

A master's thesis completed after the boundaries of our study (Sloan, 2007), also mirrored much of what we found in our research. In fact, like Hynds, it was also uncanny how close some of Sloan's conclusions came to ours. Sloan looked at writing centers across the US and Canada, using surveys and e-mail interviews with tutors and writing center directors and observations of tutoring sessions. Sloan found that experienced tutors defined a "good" tutor not by knowledge of writing or tutoring practices, but by the interpersonal dynamic. Similar to what we found, tutors in Sloan's study wanted to put their tutees "at ease" and create "a comfortable, positive atmosphere for learning" (p. 47). This personal interaction was more important than the academic aspect of the tutorial. Related to this was empathy on the tutor's part and the desire to instill confidence in the tutee. This desire for an atmosphere of comfort was expressed by every tutor in Sloan's study.

Most tutors in Sloan's study expressed a student-centered philosophy. Just as in our research, Sloan found that students were concerned with grades, correctness and mechanics. But this created a double bind for tutors who have higher-order concerns as a priority. Younger tutors identified more as peers with the students they tutored.

Mirroring our findings again, Sloan found that directive tutoring happens in practice although it's discouraged in theory. In fact, it occurs with great frequency in tutoring sessions, especially when, in the tutor's judgment, it would prove effective. The tutors were directive "to help struggling students" and "to model examples" (p. 76), but they sometimes felt guilty for using directive methods. Nevertheless, 91% of tutors in Sloan's study thought it was sometimes necessary to be directive, but they also believed that they should not tell tutees what to do, creating a double bind. As we found, Sloan also noted that tutors were more directive with

ESL students. Leading questions were seen to be a form of directivity. Tutors would always give an explanation of a grammatical correction, but students weren't always interested.

Though much of our work showed that far more happens in a tutorial session than we ever expected to discover (and especially that the personal relationship was more salient than content or techniques), not all elements of what occurs in writing centers stems from the complexities of personal interaction. Students often are the most goal-oriented of writing center participants, and many of them take a decidedly linear approach to achieving their goals. Despite the writing center commonplace that writers, not texts, are what gets improved in tutoring sessions (see North 1984a and others), the evidence suggested that writers actually do want improved texts, and writing center tutoring sessions do often focus on the improvement of student texts. Magnotto (1991) found that tutees were concerned with right and wrong and wanted to work on getting their papers right. This is in line with theoretical observations made by Shamoon and Burns (1995). Ryan (1986) found that most tutees who visited the writing center received help with grammar and usage. One of Lerner's (1996) key findings was that even students who make multiple visits to the writing center do not always alter their goal of "fixing" their essays.

We found that dyads worked on grammar when they could not find a personal connection, or when they felt uncomfortable with each other (Rodby, 2002; Ritter, 2002). Only one "negative case" was found, in which two women who were close and who liked each other worked on grammar (style) and had fun with the session (Bell, 1989b). In a more recent study not included in our data set, Block (2010) reported tutors dealing with grammar because it was "easier" or if they lacked confidence in a session they would turn to work on grammar, something that they know how to do.

Just as the needs of the student to obtain a "fixed" paper are driven by the needs of academe, so are the needs of tutors. In Gilliam's (1991) article, Belinda, the inexperienced tutor, found herself serving the needs of the academy rather than her student, Mary. (Of course she served Mary's needs, but we don't know what Mary's expectations were and whether she would see merit in

Gillam's judgment.) After all, students come to the writing center for assistance, advice, and guidance. Denying them those sorts of services is surely going to result in tutors doing lots of nothing for the betterment of the student writer. The student writer's goal is to succeed, and that tends to make the tutor-tutee exchange rather pragmatic in many, many instances. This dance of tutor and tutee needs was also noted by Hynds (1989). In her observations she stressed the need for communication and negotiation of needs, goals and stances in the tutoring session.

Likewise, Rogers (2008) found that the concerns of the administrators she studied were also goal-oriented and directive. The administrators in her study desired to have "a collaborative learning environment" and "a comfortable, non-threatening atmosphere" (p. 72), and their definitions of success included "the importance of collaboration" and "the quality of comfort and invitation" (p. 73). She also found that tutor training concerned itself with promoting "tutee self-reliance" and with the use of "questions, as opposed to direct instruction, to develop tutee understanding" (p. 111).

However, the results of Kim's (2000) study implied that the actual tutoring was a lot less collaborative and symmetrical than writing center theory would imply. This went for both NS and NNS tutees. Also, Kim suggested that more directive methods may be useful for NNS tutees. After reading Kim's dissertation, we realized that sometimes tutors do not have an understanding of the culture and language of the tutees being helped. Kim (2000) noted that Chinese students in particular do not easily opt into the reciprocal nature of Western tutoring styles. They are unaccustomed to the shared, partnered concept of peer tutoring. The implication is that NNS students respond better to a more directive style of tutoring, and that NNS may prefer a session that provides overt instruction.

Furthermore, Roswell (1992) noted that theory and practice of writing center conferences are often in conflict, and that "although writing center conferences are perceived a[s] useful and successful by student writers, they often fail to meet the expectations that conferences will be liberatory, conversational, or student-centered" (p.176); however, "...tutors with the most training were least likely to conduct highly directive conferences and [this] argues strongly for the importance of ongoing training for peer tutors" (p. 187). The bias toward non-directive tutoring is changing: We see this as a benefit to students whose needs, whether they are NS or NNS tutees, require a directive approach to addressing grammar issues.

We cannot reasonably expect tutors to understand and accommodate the cultural nuances of the world's citizens, but one of the more profound implications of our study is that tutor training must include study of culture and linguistics. Such training need not be exhaustive in order to be effective. Rogers (2008) suggested that much tutor training consisted of social dynamic training rather than training on how to teach in general, or how to teach writing in particular. She noted that tutors should be trained in "how to teach, edit, give feedback and respond" to student writing (p. 24).

Thonus (2002) found that the factors in a successful session were largely linguistic issues that were beyond conscious control, or that needed to involve both participants, so training would not seem effective, say, in telling when and if both parties should laugh or how, when, and if the tutee should accept or reject tutor suggestions. In addressing these concerns, it is important to remember that no matter who is directing the session, a tutorial session is driven by expectations based on context. Most tutors feel duty-bound to help the people who come to them, and having really only two models, teacher-centered and student-centered, we see them struggle to find the model that will most assist the student. Sometimes tutors simply adopt the model they are most comfortable with regardless of the tutee.

Grimm (2008) pointed out that the minimalist tutoring model really privileges those who are familiar with the dominant discourse and withholds "necessary cultural and linguistic information from students whose experiences and background do not match the assumptions teachers make about students" (p.10). Clearly, more can be done to bridge these gaps in discourse and to bring tutors and tutees closer together—perhaps all that is needed is some cultural competency and the knowledge that these problems exist, both of which can be included in tutor training techniques.

Closeness is a concern because, of course, the closeness of participants in a tutoring session can influence the interaction and outcome. Goody (1978) noticed that social distance and intimacy are poles on a continuum and can determine interactional choices and outcomes. Beaumont (1978) wrote that "poorly prepared tutors who do not establish a rapport with their students will not be effective in improving student writing ability" (p. 83). She defined the effective tutor as "variable in his approach, according to the needs of the student and his paper. The tutor should concentrate on playing the role—whether it is evaluator, listener or peer—that will most benefit his student, and he should be free to assume more than one role in a conference" (p. 17). Montgomery (1994) also noted the importance of tutors really listening to writers and concentrating on allowing writers to express themselves, using techniques such as questioning, encouragement and modeling proper responses in a group tutoring situation.

After closeness is established, and even when it is not, tutors and tutees take on roles based on their psychology, experience and position in or perception of academia. Beaumont listed nine possible tutor roles: Evaluator, Expert, Initiator, Interested Reader, Learner/Student, Listener, Partner in Writing, Peer and Rule-Giver (pp. 89–90). She found that the roles which resulted in the most student improvement were interested reader/listener, supportive evaluator and partner in the writing process: "Tutors who gave their students on-target criticisms, appropriate praise, and suggestions and questions rather than demands, enabled students to control their own revisions" (p. 75). Some of the other tutor behaviors she pointed out as being effective were "listening attentively," "a willingness to collaborate," "to offer suggestions as a helper" and "to participate actively in the writing process with his student." She thought that students needed a knowledge of grammar and mechanics, and that the "collaborative" tutor was most effective. She also listed comfort, interest and attentiveness as important qualities. In order to know what role is expected, the participants in the interaction must be perceptive, especially to the communication that is occurring and the possible fluidity of the role.

Likewise, Pemberton (1998) confirmed that tutees' personalities influence the session. In his study, Pemberton organized student personalities (a mixture of what we call temperament and emotion) along continua of active/passive, resistant/dependent and euphoric/depressed. The outcome of our synthesis saw the tendency for tutees to choose tutors who shared similar interests, even traits such as race or gender. Such elections, which are outside influences of personal characteristics, have a direct impact on the tutorial. Where there were discordant sessions, it was clear that such outside influences could obscure other shared or common ground. McGuire (1969) discussed liking and peerness and how people are more likely to be persuaded by people they perceive to be like them. In social psychology, it has been found that people show more liking toward that which is more familiar. Finally, previous research confirmed that positive reinforcement is key:

> An effective tutor must be able to analyze both the paper and the writer critically, but the criticism he offers must be supportive. A balance of praise and constructive criticism is that which is best received by students....An effective tutor should be able to relinquish control of the conference to the student. (Beaumont, 1978, pp. 79–80)

Severino (1992) also appeared to prefer a session in which the tutor spoke less and deferred to the plans, wishes, and outlook of the tutee. To her, this type of session was not more collaborative than a more hierarchical session, only differently collaborative.

Defining Success

While our intent was not to describe a successful session, the concept arose in our analysis and grew out of both students' concerns with obtaining "fixed papers" and the disagreements between previous researchers on the definition of success in the Writing Center. According to previous evidence-based studies, there are ways to measure the degree to which tutorial sessions are successful. They are assessments, grades, student and tutor opinions, and the evaluations of others. We are not yet in a position to determine which of these approaches is more valid, so in the spirit of describing rather than evaluating we will present some frameworks for success that occurred in our data.

Of the evidence-based studies, the work of Blau, Hall and Sparks (2002) stands out as a practical approach grounded in a method of investigating tutorials between native speaking tutors and non-native speaking tutees. Through their investigation, they came up with several guidelines for tutors:

- Tutors should have a practical grounding in contrastive rhetoric.
- Tutors should be prepared to be cultural informants as well as writing consultants.
- Tutors should be comfortable using a directive approach, especially with local concerns such as grammar, punctuation, idioms and word usage.
- Tutors should be comfortable working line-by-line through a paper, or a portion of a paper.
- Tutors can interweave global and local concerns rather than prioritizing them. If the paper's clarity is compromised by many local errors, addressing those local errors before global ones can be useful and productive.

They also made the following procedural suggestions:

- Tutors should assess the level of revision required and make a realistic plan with the client how to improve the client's writing—over multiple sessions, if necessary.
- Tutors should discuss long papers in short sections to narrow the focus of the discussion and make the reading-aloud technique more effective. (p. 42)

Thonus (2002) measured other aspccts of session success—student and tutor satisfaction—using tutorials and keying the results to discourse strategies. She found ten strategies or criteria that corresponded to successful tutorials:

- The tutor is a student, actively engaged in academic writing in his or her discipline.
- The instructor "surrogate" role is declined by the tutor, and this abdication is welcomed by the student.
- Tutor authority and expertise are not openly negotiated.
- The tutor's diagnoses and the student's self-diagnoses correspond and are agreed upon early in the session.
- Turn structure more closely resembles that of "real" conversation

> rather than an ask-and-advise service encounter comprised of restricted question + answer adjacency pairs.
>
> - Average to high rates of interactional features (volubility, overlaps, backchannels, laughter) signal involvement of both parties. Overlaps and backchannels are welcomed if they serve affiliative purposes.
> - The...tutorial [is] characterized by movements toward solidarity, including such features as simultaneous laughter, affiliative overlaps, and small talk.
> - Negotiation of acceptances and rejections of tutor evaluations and directives most often results in student acceptances. Acceptances are overt and clearly marked, and rejections, if in evidence, are supported by accounts.
> - Tutor mitigation of directives is frequent (for NS tutorials).
> - Symmetrical interpretations of discourse phases, directive forcefulness, and tutor and student behaviors contributing to success indicate that tutor and student have achieved some degree of intersubjectivity, the understanding of the other's intent. (pp. 126–129; original italics removed)

In researching another valence of success, Weigle and Nelson (2004) investigated tutoring sessions between non-native speakers and graduate students in an MA TESOL program. In the course of the limited case studies they examined, they found that tutorials with NNS writers were highly influenced by the participants' fluency in English and that the NNS tutees benefitted from directiveness, having the tutor write things down, and sharing papers in advance by email. Weigle and Nelson also mentioned the importance of rapport between tutor and tutee, but this is hard to measure.

Similarly, Blau, Hall and Strauss (1998) measured the effectiveness of tutorials through tutor and tutee feedback sheets, and they found that tutors need to be flexible, and that "an undue—or misdirected—emphasis on the collaborative [non-directive] approach resulted in tutorials that seemed to waste time and lack clear direction" (38). They also studied linguistic elements that may be beyond a tutor's conscious control, as did Mackiewicz (2004), who studied tutorials between engineering students and expert and non-expert tutors and found that tutor expertise counted to the extent that non-experts were likely to give engineering students wrong advice on their papers.

Kiedaisch and Dinitz (1993) studied several tutorials that were rated highly by both students and tutors, but were rated differently (excellent, good, and weak) by faculty raters. Due to this apparent conflict, perhaps student and tutor perception alone should not be relied upon to judge tutorial effectiveness.

While not intended to be a study on the effectiveness of specific tutoring practices, Bell (2002) found that students were more likely to be able to apply what they learned and to revise their work after a conference wherein the tutor showed them what to do and instructed them in the techniques of editing and proofreading rather than making all the changes during the conference. Harris (1995) found that tutees appreciated it when tutors allowed writers the freedom to make up their own minds rather than imposing ideas on them. Tutees also appreciated learning strategies and techniques that they could use in their writing and learning to interpret teacher comments and academic language. Writers in Harris' study also appreciated the encouragement they got from tutors.

Williams (2004) found that writers were more likely to make revisions when tutors were direct, but it was not clear that the revised drafts were any better; therefore, the effectiveness of the direct technique is questionable.

The only study that used an actual experimental design was Cumming and So (1996) who tutored non-native speakers in a 2 X 2 design with variables in the language used in the tutoring session (target or native) and session focus: error correction or "procedural facilitation," which is a sort of self-questioning heuristic. They determined success to be the ability of the tutees to take "more proactive roles in identifying, negotiating, or resolving problems in their writing" (p. 207). A specific strength they found was the shared vocabulary in the "procedural facilitation" prompts. They mention that

> a distinct benefit of one-to-one tutoring appears in tutors activating previous knowledge tuned specifically to learners' needs for improved performance, informing students of its nature, then unambiguously

> labeling it for future reference for problems of a similar type [reference omitted]. Such metacommunication about students' text revisions may, using a limited set of procedural facilitation prompts that provide a reference base of key vocabulary and models for revising writing readily comprehensible to tutors and learners alike, thus counter the logical problems commonly associated with ad hoc error correction, where an instructor's corrections can backfire if students have no way of knowing what corrections refer to or how to act on them. (p. 221)

However, the Cumming and So study pointed to the need for further research and did not supply concrete answers. Just as in Cumming and So, all the studies in this analysis have provided future scholars with a direction, if not several avenues through which one could approach an attempt to isolate and define the mechanisms of a tutorial session that results in success or failure. As the efforts of all these scholars have shown, simply using tutor and student feedback to determine if a conference was successful is anything but simple. Indeed, it can be extremely problematic. Likewise, teachers' perceptions do not always match those of students', and those do not always match those of tutors or other writing center faculty.

The area in which the results overlap is tantalizing, and in this study, we have pursued a definition of success in these areas. However, the areas in which expectations and definitions vary are also important. The varied attempts at discovering the criteria by which a successful tutorial session is defined have, thus far, shown that their results, while related, are determined by where researchers direct their attention: It is always to the particular part of the tutorial process that they have predetermined to be the most likely predictor of success. While we have attempted to avoid these pitfalls, we found that, in the end, parallel definitions of success had to be acknowledged due to their preponderance in the texts we studied. In essence, the attempt at defining the criteria of success is limited by language and by outcome-based thinking. The question remains: What is a successful tutorial session, and how can we describe its components without imposing our expectations upon a dynamic environment? And the basic question remains: How do we measure success? While this synthesis does not presume to have described every facet of the entire tutorial process as a system—we were limited by the foci of the available studies—it does posit a new method of approaching the problem of defining success—a system-based thinking that does not necessarily exclude outcome-based thinking. If a tutoring session is successful, the participants will have negotiated their own definitions of success that seem, indeed, to be simultaneously variable, but limited to a range of possible favorable outcomes. For more on definitions and measures of success, see Babcock and Thonus (2012).

Theoretical Discussion

After the analysis was complete, we turned to previously published theories to attempt to make sense out of what we found and to orient our synthesis to relevant established theories. We purposefully did not read theory before beginning so we would not be tempted to fit our data into an existing theoretical framework. Since most tutoring sessions involve two individuals, and we found that the relationship between those two individuals was arguably one of the most important aspects of the interaction, we turn now to the theory of coconstruction, as explained by Johnson, in *A Philosophy of Second Language Acquisition* (2004):

> The notion of coconstruction releases the individual from his or her sole responsibility for conducting a successful and appropriate interaction for a given social context. The responsibility is shared by all participants. Also, in the theory of interactional competence, meaning does not exist independent of social reality. It is not fixed in advance. Meaning is negotiated through face-to-face interaction and is jointly coconstructed in a locally bound social context. (p. 97)

We can see that in a tutoring situation, the participants are coconstructors of the event, and the writing tutorial is a classic situation in which participants' social interaction is "the locus in which culture and cognition create each other" (Jacoby & Ochs, 1995, p. 173). This social constructivist theory is well-supported in writing center practice, but it is still in conflict with the Romantic version of the writer as all-knowing and the tutor as selfless facilitator, there to draw out the writer's ideas. Lunsford (1991) called this the garret writing center model. In the studies we examined, the participants supported each other and together created a discourse situation in which both could learn and both could be transformed. Of course, this didn't always happen, and there were some failed interactions.

Regarding the tutor as authority figure, no matter what we may wish to have happen in an idealized tutoring session, it is inevitable that the tutee will sometimes view the tutor as having more expertise. That is, after all, why the tutee has come to the tutor—to gain knowledge that they feel they lack. Clearly, there are exceptions, as in some required visits to a writing center, but even then, the tendency is for the tutee to confer on the tutor a status above the tutee's own. Granting elevated status on the part of the tutee is in part environmental. The tutee usually visits a particular space designated for the tutorial. The space itself confers institutional status on the tutor. As part of the operations of the university, the tutor is him- or herself an institutional functionary (Thonus, 1999a).

Vygotsky's theories also are quite relevant to our findings. Vygotsky wrote that "Social relations or relations among people genetically underline all higher functions and their relationships" (1981, p. 163). This could also help us in our understanding of the tutoring process. Johnson (2004) wrote about a study by Donato in which "construction of knowledge results in major linguistic change among and within the individual learners: this developmental change is not individual, but social in nature" (p. 130). Johnson goes on to explain Vygotsky's theories that might be helpful for us in making sense of our study:

> The construct of Vygotsky's Z[one of] P[roximal] D[evelopment] specifies that learning cannot occur if too much assistance is provided or if a problem-solving task is too easy. Helping too much or withdrawing help from the learner too soon impedes the process of development. The responsibility for providing the appropriate level of assistance to the learner is predicated both on the interlocutor's sensitivity to the learner's needs and the interlocutor's ability to withdraw assistance when it is not needed. (p. 141)

The concept of scaffolding, something we think of as a learning process that occurs when an expert/novice, parent/child, or other similar dyad work together to improve the skill of the less knowledgeable partner, is related to the Zone of Proximal Development. In Vygotsky's work, this is the skill level just beyond the novice's abilities. The novice is not quite able to go to the next level or next skill set without assistance. Through dialogical psychosocial interplay between partners, the novice can perform above his or her skill level with the assistance of an expert or more capable peer, even when the expert does little beyond merely observing. Our understanding of the Zone of Proximal Development is that it is not a theory about how to help or how much to help, but simply describes the level a child (or a learner) can achieve with help, which is almost always a higher level than he or she can achieve alone.

As the learning process continues, the novice seems more sensitive to previous instruction, and through a complex interplay of internal dialog and private speech, the novice begins to approximate the skill that lies just outside his or her expertise. The pedagogical use of this in group work is based on the idea of scaffolding, or building vertically toward the ideal goal, with the teacher/expert providing guidance as needed: "[I]n social interaction a knowledgeable participant can create, by means of speech, supportive conditions in which the novice can participate in, and extend, current skills and knowledge to higher levels of competence" (Donato, 1994, p. 40).

According to Wood, Bruner and Ross (1984), "scaffolded help is characterized by six features":

1. recruiting interest in the task,
2. simplifying the task,
3. maintaining pursuit of the goal,
4. marking critical features and discrepancies between what has been produced and the ideal solution,
5. controlling frustration during problem solving, and
6. demonstrating an idealized version of the act to be performed. (qtd in Donato, 1994, pp. 40–41)

Donato's thesis is that scaffolding can occur without the presence of an expert: It can occur among novices. How does this apply to writing center tutorials? We know that there is a strong, almost obdurate tendency among tutees to view tutors as experts. We know also that tutors who are instructed in student-centered, non-directive tutorial methods resist the expert role. We have seen in various transcripts of tutorials the interplay of a non-directive tutor with a tutee as they explore an issue. When the tutee freely allows the tutor to adopt the non-directive approach, we see a form of scaffolding in their interaction. We have sometimes referred to this in our research as negotiation.

Negotiation is more accurately a scaffolding event when the tutor and tutee discuss higher order concerns as opposed to the default position of mechanics and grammar. Support for this is convincing when we remind ourselves of the murkiness of authorial intent. Only the tutee has expertise in that regard, while the tutor has expertise in writing. Furthermore, the tutor may not be a more skilled writer than the tutee—which so far has been a non-factor in our study.

Nevertheless, it is possible to witness scaffolding events in more directive tutorials. Very little attention was paid to positive directive tutorials in the various studies we found, so there is little available documented evidence. This is likely more a function of ideological bias than reality. Lerner (1996) found that when tutor and tutee expectations meshed, there was more possibility for Vygotskian scaffolding to occur. For ESL learners, we have also seen scaffolding when grammar and mechanics were the focus of learning.

We have many instances of private speech occurrences in tutorials as one or both of the partners speak as though to themselves. We see also the six steps of scaffolding on display as the tutor engages the tutee in the discussion, simplification of the task and all the rest, including and especially at times, controlling frustration. If the task becomes too difficult, the fallback position is almost always grammar, an objective subject which is governed by concrete rules. We might therefore conclude that much of what we have found to occur in writing tutorials is a Vygotskian scaffolding event. Less successful tutoring sessions often result because the negotiation of roles is less successful—and this can occur for a maddeningly large amount of reasons. Success seems to be contingent upon preconceptions and expectations developed outside the actual tutorial. These can be overcome in many instances, the evidence of which is substantial in our project. However, the tutor's and tutee's abilities to negotiate roles are vital to the success of the session and to their perceptions of the session's success.

Just as Vygotsky (1978) noted that children needed to use speech when performing tasks beyond their level of difficulty, it seems that adolescents and adults may also need to use speech to "talk it out" when trying to perform difficult tasks, like writing academic papers. The writing center tutorial is based, implicitly, on this theory: The use of talk is needed to accomplish difficult tasks. Vygotsky (1978) also discussed children planning a course of action using speech, which also occurs in the writing center when people brainstorm and discuss what they are going to write about. An experiment done by Vygotsky demonstrated the necessity of the tutor to the writing process, if adolescents and adults are anything like children when trying to solve difficult problems. In this experiment, when the child attempted a task and ran into a problem, she would ask the experimenter for help. Vygotsky wrote, "By asking a question, the child indicates that he has, in fact, formulated a plan to solve the task before him, but is unable to perform all the necessary operations" (p. 29). This sounds very much like a writer seeking help in a writing center.

Furthermore, Storch (2002) produced an interesting matrix that may inform analyses of tutoring. This matrix has high and low mutuality on one axis and low and high equality on the other. She names the quadrants, clockwise from upper left "expert/novice, collaborative, dominant/dominant, and dominant/passive." Storch found that learning most likely occurred with the collaborative and novice/expert pairs.

Lastly, Aljaafreh and Lantolf (1994) presented a study that unfortunately has gone under-cited in writing center literature. They explained that scaffolding help can be offered on a continuum, and that directive/non-directive are not binaries, but rather poles on a scale with many gradations. In their study of tutoring, they provided twelve steps of help that a tutor can give, from no help at all, to very specific assistance:

0. Tutor asks the learner to read, find the errors, and correct them independently, prior to the tutorial.

1. Construction of a "collaborative frame" prompted by the presence of the tutor as a potential dialogic partner.

2. Prompted or focused reading of the sentence that contains the error by the learner or the tutor.

3. Tutor indicates that something may be wrong in a segment (e.g., sentence, clause, line)—"Is there anything wrong with this sentence?"

3. Tutor rejects the unsuccessful attempts at recognizing the error.

4. Tutor narrows down the location of the error (e.g., tutor repeats or points to the specific segment which contains the error).

5. Tutor indicates the nature of the error, but does not identify the error (e.g., "There is something wrong with the tense marking here").

6. Tutor identifies the error ("You can't use an auxiliary here").

7. Tutor rejects learner's unsuccessful attempts at correcting the error.

8. Tutor provides clues to help the learner arrive at the correct form (e.g., "It is not really past but something that is still going on").

9. Tutor provides the correct form.

10. Tutor provides some explanation for the use of the correct form.

11. Tutor provides examples of the correct pattern when other forms of help fail to produce an appropriate responsive action. (p. 471)

These examples are specifically to be used to correct surface form for non-native speakers, but they could also be modified to be used in other ways as well.

Implications

The implications of our study, we hope, will serve as points of departure for other scholars who wish to use similar grounded-theory approaches to describe writing center tutoring or other types of phenomena. With further research, it may be possible to achieve a true laboratory approach to navigating through the once-vague details of tutoring (Lerner, 2006). The developing approach may not be completely scientific in a positivist, modernist sense, but it will be bounded by the limits of human behavior, psychology, and the real needs of tutees and tutors.

That said, proscriptive, tutor-centered instruction may work, but it has profound drawbacks. Some students, tutors and directors may want a homogenized academic voice to meet expectations of professors, but many also value the original, fresh voice that comes from students seeking to express their experiences. Insisting that students adhere to the monotone of academic writing surely blights the genuine originality that they might bring to the conversation, yet we still struggle to strike a balance between these voices. This was Belinda's experience (Gilliam, 1991). The ideas inspired in Gillam by Bakhtin might actually result in the freewheeling and writer-enhancing sessions she envisioned, but, in this synthesis, we have seen minimalism and proscription falter, fail, and frustrate repeatedly. We are then left to explore a middle ground rooted in collaboration.

However, the term "collaboration" has the potential to be misunderstood or applied haphazardly as a synonym for "success," a polyseme too elastic to be instructive. Perhaps as researchers, we should coin a new word rather than using potentially loaded words that, though they denote some kind of synthesis of communication and cooperation, could be understood to mean whatever the readers already understand them to mean according to their theoretical approaches of choice. Maybe "Vygoskiation" for instance, would be a more apt term. "Scaffolding," while it comes close, is not quite as apt a descriptor. We fear that "collaboration" or any other word used to replace it will end up being a synonym for a successful conference, because having a successful conference is sometimes, but not always, a result of collaboration. Truly, success is the result of the participants' successful negotiation of their dynamic roles in the session. So, if we are to begin with a subjective interpretation of success, a successful conference to a student is related to outcome, such as getting that fixed paper and getting out of the writing center in time for the next class. The student could be happy with the end result and the tutor could feel that the student cooperated and provided enough feedback to justify calling the session a successful one. If this is considered a successful session, it was accomplished without much collaboration, especially if the student simply wanted a fixed paper and the tutor did most of the work. This is but one example of how a session can achieve a type of success without collaboration.

Accepted writing center philosophy dictates that tutors minimize their impact on the student's work by avoiding things like supplying phrases, sentences, or even a single word that the student writer did not generate. As we frequently found in the data, however, what really happened was quite different from either the instructor's expectations (here we mean academe in general) or the expectations of writing center practitioners who are invested in the received wisdom of writing center dogma. As many writing center professionals have already acknowledged, the data showed us that minimalist tutoring does not work for many students. Although some in writing centers may believe that non-directive tutoring is dead, or is now a non-issue, in reality the debate still rages on (Corbett, 2008). In light of this, especially where NNS tutees are concerned, the tutor's directive instruction may violate currently accepted notions of plagiarism even when keeping within the spirit of academic honesty. Perhaps this definition needs to be re-examined. Students who cannot recognize their errors and whose self-correcting heuristics are either underdeveloped or faulty will need direct correction if they are to gain the reinforcement they need to be able to proceed into non-directive tutoring; this situation is quite different from that of the NS student whose self-correcting heuristic leads him or her to the appropriate section in a grammar book without first being reminded of where to look or why.

Since success is so relative and collaboration is multifaceted, if there is apparent collaboration in a successful session, we must ask ourselves how we can assure ourselves of the participants' authenticity. Here, we would delve into the psychology of learning and interpersonal communication strategies, though it is simpler to not worry about such details than it would be to break out the brain-scanners and polygraph machines. Maybe our trouble with collaboration and its relationship to a successful session is a good place to inject a suggestion for further research. The value of the word and concept of "collaboration" in writing center discourse probably stems from the value of the social constructivist position as the default or expected writing center theory (beginning with Bruffee, 1984 and further articulated in Lunsford, 1991), and the place and necessity of collaboration and collaborative learning to this theoretical position.

Indeed, "collaboration" cannot and should not be synonymous with success. It is increasingly imperative that writing center theory and practice address the pragmatics of life in an era when assessment is not an optional add-on, but a requirement for existence. That is, writing centers need to be able to demonstrate success in concrete terms, and those terms must include student outcomes and student retention, the basic markers of success. So, while we may approach tutorials from a variety of philosophical or pedagogical vantages, we need to assess outcomes from a more practical reality while attempting to reconcile the necessities of reality with the necessities of academic honesty and sound pedagogical practices. A follow-up comparative study that considered the relative success or failure of programs based on their theoretical and pedagogical approach seems to be the next logical step—we need to discover what works best. Next, we must re-examine the path we have taken to learn the reason why it works.

This study describes how tutoring is actually conducted in writing centers, revealing both effective and ineffective practices, and resulting in quite a few implications for tutor training and practice. For instance, the results of Bell's (1999) study of a possibly learning-disabled student points out the obvious need for training tutors in various learning disabilities. The tutor in this study admitted that she didn't know anything about dyslexia, and the session could possibly have been enhanced if the tutor had had training in learning disabilities. Blau, Hall and Sparks (2002), Thonus (2003) and Hunzer (1997) made recommendations for tutor training as the result of their studies. For instance, Hunzer suggested that tutees be allowed to choose the gender of their tutor, so they could be comfortable with whom they are working. She also suggested that tutors ask students what they prefer to work on, and to encourage tutors to work on a variety of styles so they will not fall into stereotyped roles, i.e., females as caring and males as aggressive.

Finally, Thompson, Whyte, Shannon, Muse, Miller, Chappell et al. (2009) looked at both lore-based and research-based aspects of tutoring sessions and found that session feedback linked to satisfaction supported the lore that the writing tutorial was a place to make students feel comfortable and for answering their questions. Aspects of "peerness" or time at talk were not important. Their results implied that tutees desire expertise on the part of tutors, and not necessarily a strictly peer-to-peer collaboration. Thompson et al. found that some directiveness may be necessary, and also that students were interested in improving their drafts and their grades. These findings were in line with those of Kiedaisch and Dinitz (1993) who found that tutors sometimes needed to be experts, and at the same time needed to balance being too directive or not directive enough.

Though these works, when combined, may seem contradictory, it is only an appearance achieved at a glance. What writing center scholars have been pointing toward is efficacy, and, in our study, we hope to have begun the process of revealing what techniques are the most efficacious and why they are so. The discord of voices acclaiming directive and non-directive approaches can achieve harmony through the simple realization that, in the circumstances in which each technique was found to work, that technique was likely the best suited for the circumstance. Though each method may still warrant more study, the fact that they are components of a larger system of tutoring that is based on the idea that tutoring must meet the needs of the tutees is essential to understanding tutoring as a whole. There may be no one way in which human beings learn best, in general. If that is true, then our task is to seek knowledge of the specific ways in which some human beings learn and to expand our knowledge continually until systems begin to appear, to become internally cogent and to be obviously dissimilar from one another. Ideally, tutors should be trained to recognize and to adapt to each tutee's individual learning needs and preferences—our categories of Personal Characteristics, Emotion and Temperament. Only then will we be able to prescribe methods of learning to the individuals to whom they are best suited—and the goal seems far off. There are too many strategies for participants to use and too many reasons—such as outside influences that may be out of the participants' control—why they may succeed or fail when it comes to the ultimate outcome of the tutoring session. No matter what the future holds for writing center theory, however, tutors have always needed and will always need to be adaptable, and, at the bare minimum, by emphasizing adaptability, cooperation, and the acceptance of and adaptation to different learning styles, we can do our part to prepare pedagogy for a leap forward.

In summation, many of the above comments are our considered opinions after conducting this work, rather than direct results of the study. What our study achieved was a theoretical understanding of what is involved in *all* tutoring sessions, with no judgments, opinions or evaluations involved: Two people with unique personal characteristics come together in a situation rife with outside influences, many beyond their control. They communicate, and this communication is mediated by their personal characteristics and the roles they assume, as well as their emotions and temperament. These factors determine the outcome of the session which includes the session focus, the participants' relationship, and material outcomes. So a student-centered tutorial—and our data shows us they are quite rare—does not just occur on its own. All the above factors, which are many times uncontrollable and unpredictable, contribute to the ultimate shape of the session.

Looking Toward the Future

Thompson et al. wrote, "over the past twenty years, empirical research has shown the limitations or inaccuracy of some lore-based mandates and has provided support for others." Namely, research from the past two decades has shown that "tutors are unable to avoid directiveness" and this directiveness is "often appreciated by students" (2009, p. 79). Furthermore, naïveté on the part of tutors was not desirable to students: They wanted experts or semi-experts who could answer their questions, seemingly discarding one of the factors that builds peerness—a shared experience as students in the college environment. As our research and that of others has shown, tutees often confer an expert status to tutors whether or not the tutors desire it. It appears that further research is trending in this direction, or, at least, writing center scholars are discovering that, as far as tutoring methods are concerned, there is evidence of an excluded middle approach. Sloan (2007) suggested that writing center researchers change their focus from whether or not to be directive, to "*to what extent* and *under what circumstances* tutors are directive" (p. 115, emphasis original).

So, where can this line of inquiry lead in the future? Thompson et al. have already given us a sign. They based their work upon Ede and Lunsford's distinction between dialogic and hierarchical collaboration, writing that, in a writing center setting, dialogic collaboration would be considered "true" collaboration and the opposite of hierarchical collaboration. Just as we did in this study, Thompson et al. (2009) found that there is rigidity in both modes of collaboration because they are binary; it has been thought that there can be no such thing as semi-hierarchical collaboration that is directive without requiring submission or semi-dialogic collaboration that calls for cooperation with an expert. Thompson et al. (2009) called this excluded third means of collaboration "asymmetrical collaboration." It is a collaboration style in which both the student and the tutor have power, and dialog is established along the lines of expert-novice roles, as in Vygotskian scaffolding. In this model, the tutor has greater expertise in the subject, but the student has the power to initiate the collaboration and set the agenda. The tutor's directiveness is based on the student's needs and expectations, and the tutor is responsible for making the student "feel comfortable enough to take risks" (p. 97) and develop and maintain the motivation to complete the task.

What makes the Thompson et al. study unique is that it was based on empirical data collected at Auburn University using survey data in the form of a six-point Likert scale expressed using a Pearson Product-Moment Correlation that described the relationship between components of the tutorial session and overall satisfaction. The conference attributes were, compared to ours, limited. They were students' comfort, students' questions answered, tutors' expertise, positive feedback, tutors as peers more than instructors, nondirectiveness, how much students talked, and conference satisfaction.

The results of the Thompson et al. study, however, were very similar to ours. Whereas they discovered empirical data that suggested a similar course of action to what we suggest, our synthesis of 23 years of writing center scholarship caused us to arrive at the same conclusion by standing on the shoulders of others. One complements the other, and, since our group and Thompson's were both working on our respective projects without any knowledge of each other at approximately the same time (Thompson et al. had likely already begun to work while we were presenting in 2007), could it be that the move toward a synthesis of old and new writing center practices is in the pedagogical zeitgeist?

Independent minds arriving at nearly identical conclusions that question the effectiveness of practices based in writing center lore surely indicate a developing trend in scholarship; something about writing center lore is no longer helping our students and, given the wide variance in theory vs. practice, may never have been effective aides to writing center clients. Since helping our students is precisely why the lore developed, it is time for our methods to evolve. This development need not be stifling or overwhelming. The lore is correct in telling us that students need freedom to develop their voices, but they also need guidance—they're asking us for guidance—and if we cannot or will not answer their questions, we may be of no more value to them than the proverbial wise man on the mountain who replies to those who seek him, "The meaning of life? Go figure it out for yourself!" since not all writers share the writing center's vision of creative freedom. Some simply want a product—in the end, a grade, and feel that they have been quite creative enough.

Where research must move in the future is toward articulating new methods of tutoring that use complementary features from the ways of the old grammarians and the techniques of writing teachers who want their students to focus on self-expression. Students want to be "correct" and want "fixed" papers, and although we may debate about whether or not the correction they seek stifles their voices, we must trust that our students are asking for something that they genuinely want and need—instruction that they already wish to use to improve their writing skills. Whether the directive component of tutoring makes a reappearance in its native form or whether it must adapt to current lore will be the domain of the scholars who write after these studies that propose searching for a middle way in tutoring. In summary, our suggestion for further research is work that builds on Thompson's—and ours. It will be research that changes the face of writing center tutoring as we know it. The writing center stands in the breach between campus Romantics and Pragmatists, thus, its ever-changing and always controversial position as both a fixer of papers and an improver of writers. Only by acknowledging the writing center's unique role to play in the academic community and the flexibility and rigidity it can offer to writers, as they need either, can we begin to reach toward a more definitive understanding of what occurs in writing center tutorial sessions.

APPENDIX

Inclusion Criteria Matrix

	No (0)	Low (1)	Moderate (2)	High (3)
Is the study a qualitative analysis?				
Does it include primary data?				
Are the methods clearly described?				
Is data collection appropriate to our needs (ie., qualitative) ?				
Is method of data analysis clear?				
What is the general quality of the study?				
Is there evidence of research bias?				
Is the context a college writing center?				
Is tutoring the focus of the study?				

BIBLIOGRAPHY

Aljaafreh, A. & Lantolf, J. P. (1994). Negative feedback as regulation and second language learning in the Zone of Proximal Development. *The Modern Language Journal, 78*, 465–483.

*Babcock, R. D. (2005). Tutoring deaf students in the writing center. *Dissertation Abstracts International: Section A, Humanities and Social Sciences, 66*(03), 980.

Babcock, R. D., Manning, K., McCain, A., & Rogers, T. (2007). A synthesis of qualitative studies of writing center tutoring. Paper presented at the conference of the International Writing Centers Association, Houston.

Babcock, R. D., & Thonus, T. (2012). *Researching the writing center: Towards an evidence-based practice.* New York: Peter Lang.

Banning, J. H. (n.d.) Ecological triangulation: An approach for qualitative meta-synthesis. Retrieved November 18, 2005 from http://new.soe.cahs.colostate.edu/faculty/jimbanning/PDFs/Ecological%20Triangualtion.pdf

*Bean, J. (1998). Conversation and gender in a university composition program. *Dissertation Abstracts International: Section A, Humanities and Social Sciences, 60*(02), 409.

*———. (1999) Feminine discourse in the university: The writing center conference as a site of linguistic resistance. *Feminist empirical research: Emerging perspectives on qualitative and teacher research.* Ed. Joanne Addison and Sharon James McGee. Portsmouth, NH: Boynton/Cook. 127–144.

Beaumont, P. A. (1978). *A descriptive study of the role of the tutor in a conference on writing.* (Unpublished master's thesis.) University of San Diego, San Diego, CA.

*Bell, D. C. & Youmans, M. (2006). Politeness and praise: Rhetorical issues in ESL (L2) writing center conferences. *Writing Center Journal, 26*(2), 31–47.

Bell, J. (1989a). What are we talking about?: A content analysis of the *Writing Lab Newsletter*, April 1985 to October 1998. *Writing Lab Newsletter, 13*(7), 1–5.

*———. (1989b). *Tutoring in a writing center.* Doctoral Dissertation: University of Texas at Austin. Available from ProQuest Dissertations and Theses database. (UMI 9005528)

*———. (1999). Tutoring a provisional student in composition. *Journal of College Reading and Learning, 29*(2), 194–208.

*Blau, S. R., Hall, J., Davis, J., & Gravitz, L. (2001). Tutoring ESL students: A different kind of session. *Writing Lab Newsletter, 25*(10), 1–4.

*Blau, S., Hall, J., & Sparks, S. (2002). Guilt-free tutoring: Rethinking how we tutor non-native-English-speaking students. *Writing Center Journal, 23*(1), 3–44.

*Blau, S. R., Hall, J., and Strauss, T. (1998). Exploring the tutor/client conversation: A linguistic analysis. *Writing Center Journal, 19*(1), 19–49.

Block, R. (2010). *Reading aloud in the writing center: A comparative analysis of three tutoring methods.* (Doctoral dissertation) Available from ProQuest Dissertations and Theses database. (UMI No. 3415200)

Bloom, B. S. (1984). The 2 sigma problem: Searching for methods of group instruction as effective as one-on-one tutoring. *Educational Researcher, 13* (6), 4–16.

*Boudreaux, M. A. (1998). Toward awareness: A study of nonverbal behavior in the writing conference. *Dissertation Abstracts International, Section A. Humanities and Social Sciences, 59*(04), 1145.

*Briggs, L. C. (1991). *Writing center talk in a long-term writer-consultant relationship.* Doctoral dissertation, Syracuse University. UMI No. 9204493

Bruffee, K. A. (1984). Peer tutoring and the "conversation of mankind." In G. A. Olson (Ed.), *Writing centers: Theory and administration* (pp. 3–15). Urbana, IL: NCTE.

*Callaway, S. (1993). Collaboration, resistance and the authority of the student writer. *Dissertation Abstracts International, Section A. Humanities and Social Sciences, 54*(07), 2555.

*Cardenas, D. (2000). The conversation of the consultation: Describing collaborations. *Dissertation Abstracts International, Section A. Humanities and Social Sciences, 61*(11), 4368.

*Carter-Tod, S. L. (1995). *The role of the writing center in the writing practice of L2 students.* (Doctoral dissertation: Virginia Polytechnic Institute).

Clark, I. L., & Healy, D. (1996). Are writing centers ethical? *WPA*, 20(1-2).

*Cogie, J. (2001). Peer tutoring: Keeping the contradiction productive. In J. Nelson and K. Evertz (Eds.). *The politics of writing centers* (pp. 37–49). Portsmouth, NH: Boynton/Cook.

*———. (2006). ESL student participation in writing center sessions. *Writing Center Journal, 26*(2), 48–66.

*Cook-Gumperz, J. (1993). Dilemmas of identity: Oral and written literacies in the making of a basic writing student. *Anthropology and Education Quarterly, 24,* 336–356.

Cooper, H. M. & Lindsay, J. J. (1998). Research synthesis and meta-analysis. In L. Bickman & D. J. Rog (Eds.), *Handbook of applied social research methods* (pp. 315–337). Thousand Oaks, CA: Sage.

Corbett, S. J. (2008). Tutoring style, tutoring ethics: The continuing relevance of the directive/nondirective instructional debate. *Praxis: A Writing Center Journal, 5*(2). Available from http://projects.uwc.utexas.edu/praxis/?q=node/200.

Cumming, A., & So, S. (1996). Tutoring second language text revision: Does the approach to instruction or the language of communication make a difference? *Journal of Second Language Writing, 5,* 197–226. Retrieved June 1, 2009 from Science Direct database.

David, C. & Bubolz, T. (1985). Evaluating students' achievement in a writing center. *Writing Lab Newsletter, 9*(8), 10–14.

Dick, B. (n.d.) Grounded theory: A thumbnail sketch. *Resource papers in action research.* Retrieved November 11, 2005 from http://www.scu.edu.au/schools/gcm/ar/arp/grounded.html

*DiPardo, A. (1992). "Whispers of coming and going": Lessons from Fannie. *Writing Center Journal, 12*(2), 125–144.

Donato, R. (1994). Collective scaffolding in second language learning. In J. P. Lantolf & G. Appel (Eds.), *Vygotskian approaches to second language research* (pp. 33–56). Norwood, NJ: Ablex.

*Eckard, S. J. (2001). Storytelling in composition classrooms and writing centers. *Dissertation Abstracts International: Section A. Humanities, 62*(09), 3033.

Fallon, B. (2010). *The perceived, conceived, and lived experiences of 21st century peer writing tutors.* (Doctoral dissertation). Retrieved from http://dspace.iup.edu/handle/2069/1

Ferster, T. (1937). An English laboratory for freshmen. *English Journal, 27,* 729–734.

*Fletcher, D. C. (1993). On the issue of authority. In T. Flynn & M. King (Eds.) *Dynamics of the writing conference: Social and cognitive interactions* (pp. 41–50). Urbana, IL: NCTE.

*Fox, C. M. (2003). Writing across cultures: Contrastive rhetoric and a writing center study of one student's journey. *Dissertation Abstracts International: Section A. Humanities, 65*(07), 2589.

*Frank, L. (1983). The writing lab at work: Two case studies. In M. Harris & T. Baker (Eds.), *New directions, new connections: Proceedings of the Writing Centers Association fifth conference.* West Lafayette, IN: Department of English, Purdue University.

Gillam, A. M. (1991). Writing center ecology: A Bakhtinian perspective. *Writing Center Journal, 11*(2), 3–13.

Grimm, N. (2008). Attending to the change potential of writing center narratives. *Writing Center Journal, 28*(1), 3–21.

Goody, E. N. (1978). *Questions and politeness.* Cambridge, UK: Cambridge University Press.

*Haas, T. S. (1986). A case study of peer tutors' writing conferences with students: Tutors' roles and conversations about composing. *Dissertation Abstracts International: Section A, Humanities and Social Sciences, 47*(12), 4309.

*Harris, M. (1995). Talking in the middle: Why writers need writing tutors. *College English, 57*(1), 27–43.

Highlen, P. S. & Finley, H. C. (1996). Doing qualitative analysis. In F. T. L. Leong & J. T. Austin (Eds.), *The psychology research handbook* (pp. 177–192). Thousand Oaks, CA: Sage.

*Hemmeter, T. & Mee, C. (1993). The writing center as ethnographic space. *Writing Lab Newsletter, 18*(3), 4–5.

Horner, W. (1929). The economy of the laboratory method. *The English Journal, 18,* 214–221.

*Hunter, K. R. (1993) Tutor talk: A study of selected linguistic factors affecting tutor-writer interaction in a university writing center. *Dissertation Abstracts International: Section A, Humanities and Social Sciences, 54*(10), 3727

*Hunzer, K. (1997). Misperceptions of gender in the writing center: Stereotyping and the facilitative tutor. *Writing Lab Newsletter, 22*(2), 6–10.

Hynds, S. (1989). Perspectives on perspectives in the writing center conference. *Focuses, 2*(2), 77–90.

Jacoby, S. & Ochs, E. (1995) Co-construction: An introduction. *Research on Language and Social Interaction, 28*, 171–183

Jones, C. (2001). The relationship between writing centers and the improvement of writing ability: A review of the literature. *Education, 122*, 3–20.

Johnson, J. B. (1993). Reevaluation of the question as a teaching tool. In T. Flynn & M. King (Eds.), *Dynamics of the writing conference* (pp. 34–40). Urbana, IL: NCTE.

Johnson, M. (2004). *A philosophy of second language acquisition.* New Haven, CT: Yale University Press.

*Johnstone, A. (1989). The writing tutorial as ecology: A case study. *Writing Center Journal, 9*(2), 51–57.

*Jordan, K. S. (2003). *Power and empowerment in writing center conferences.* (Doctoral dissertation). Retrieved from http://etd.lsu.edu/docs/available/etd-0407103-143704/

*Kiedaisch, J. and Dinitz, S. (1993). Look back and say "so what": The limitations of the generalist tutor. *Writing Center Journal, 14*(1), 63–74.

*Kim, Y.-K. (2000). Frame analysis of NS-NS and NS-NNS discourse in university writing center tutorials: Volubility and questions. *Dissertation Abstracts International: Section A. Humanities and Social Sciences, 62*(1), 145.

*Lerner, N. (1996). Teaching and learning in a university writing center. *Dissertation Abstracts International: Section A, Humanities and Social Sciences, 57*(3), 1060.

———. (2006). Time warp: Historical representations of writing center directors. In C. Murphy and B. L. Stay (Eds.). *The writing center director's resource book.* (pp. 3–11). Mahwah, NJ: Lawrence Erlbaum.

———. (2009). *The idea of a writing laboratory.* Carbondale: Southern Illinois University Press.

Lunsford, A. (1991). Collaboration, control, and the idea of a writing center. *Writing Center Journal, 12*(1), 3–11

*Mackiewicz, J. M. (2001). The Co-construction of social relationships in writing center tutoring interactions: An analysis of politeness strategies in discourse activity frames. *Dissertation Abstracts International: Section A, Humanities and Social Sciences, 62*(12), 4145.

*Magnotto, J. N. (1991). The constructions of college writing in a cross-disciplinary, community college writing center: An analysis of student, tutor and faculty representations *Dissertation Abstracts International: Section A, Humanities and Social Sciences, 52*(07), 2382.

*McClure, S. H. (1990). An observational study of the behavior of first semester college students as tutors in a writing center. *Dissertation Abstracts International: Section A, Humanities and Social Sciences, 51*(03), 0193.

McGuire, W. J. (1969). The nature of attitude change. In G. Lindzey and E. Aronson (Eds.), *The handbook of social psychology.* 2nd ed. Vol. 3 (pp. 136–314). Reading, MA: Addison-Wesley.

*McInerney, K. H. (1998). *A portrait of one writing center through undergraduate tutors' talk: Themes of home, heart, and head.* (Doctoral Dissertation, University of Iowa).

*Melnick, J. F. (1984). The politics of writing conferences: Describing authority through Speech Act Theory. *Writing Center Journal, 4*(2), 9–21.

Montgomery, N. (1994). Facilitating talk about text in small writing groups. *Focuses, 7*(2), 79–88.

Moore, R. H. (1950). The writing clinic and the writing laboratory. *College English, 11*, 388–393.

*Moser, A. H. (2002). Theories, techniques, and the impacts of computer-mediated conferencing in a university writing center: Toward a model for training programs. *Dissertation Abstracts International: Section A, Humanities and Social Sciences, 65*(12), 4451.

*Murphy, S. W. (2001). Politeness and self-presentation in writing center discourse. *Dissertation Abstracts International: Section A, Humanities and Social Sciences, 62*(11), 3766.

*———. (2006). "Just chuck it: I mean, don't get fixed on it": Self presentation in writing center discourse." *Writing Center Journal, 26*(1), 62–82.

*Nicolas, M. (2002). Re-telling the story: An exploration of the feminization of the writing center narrative. *Dissertation Abstracts International: Section A, Humanities and Social Sciences, 63*(07), 2529.

North, S. (1984a). The idea of a writing center. *College English, 46,* 433–446.

———. (1984b). Writing center research: Testing our assumptions. In G. Olson, Ed. *Writing centers: Thoory and administration.* (pp. 24–35). Urbana, IL: NCTE.

Pemberton, M. A. (1998). Tutorial ethics: Student personalities. *Writing Lab Newsletter, 23*(1), 10–12.

Reis, S., Hermoni, D., Van-Raalte, R., Dahan, R., & Borkan, J. (2002, November). Meta-synthesis of qualitative studies: From theory to practice. Paper presented at the 30th annual meeting of the North American Primary Care Research Group, Providence, RI. Retrieved from http://www.napcrg.org/2002handouts/j3.ppt

*Ritter, J. J. (2002). Negotiating the center: An analysis of writing tutorial interactions between ESL learners and native-English speaking writing center tutors. *Dissertation Abstracts International, Section A. Humanities and Social Sciences, 63*(6), 2224.

*Robertson, K. S. (2005). Technology and the role of peer tutors: How writing center tutors perceive the experience of online tutoring. *Dissertation Abstracts International: Section A, Humanities and Social Sciences, 66*(02), 580.

*Rodby, J. (2002). The subject is literacy: General education and the dialectics of power and resistance in the writing center. In P. Gillespie, A. Gillam, L. F. Brown & B. Stay (Eds.) *Writing center research* (pp. 221–234). Mahwah, NJ: Lawrence Erlbaum.

Rogers, K. S. (2008). *Investigating tutor training and evaluation practices in colleges and universities in the Mid-Atlantic region.* (Doctoral Dissertation.) Available from ProQuest Dissertations and Theses database. (UMI No. 3294805)

*Roswell, B. S. (1992). The tutor's audience is always a fiction: The construction of authority in writing center conferences. *Dissertation Abstracts International: Section A, Humanities and Social Sciences, 53*(11), 3830.

Ryan, A. L. K. (1986). An investigation and description of some relationships between tutorial assistance in a writing center and the writing apprehension of freshman composition students. *Dissertation Abstracts International, Section A. Humanities and Social Sciences, 47*(08), 2930.

*Seckendorf, M. H. (1986). Writing center conferences: An analysis. *Dissertation Abstracts International: Section A, Humanities and Social Sciences, 47*(08), 3024.

*Severino, C. (1992). Rhetorically analyzing collaborations. *Writing Center Journal, 13*(1), 53–64.

Shamoon, L. K. & Burns, D. H. (1995). A critique of pure tutoring. *Writing Center Journal, 15*(2), 134–151.

Sloan, P. (2007). *Contextualizing writing centers.* (Unpublished MA Thesis, Carleton University).

*Stachera, S. A. (2003). Tongue tied: Coming to terms with our writing center practice. *Dissertation Abstracts International: Section A, Humanities and Social Sciences, 64*(12), 4450.

Strauss, A. & Corbin, J. (1994). Grounded theory methodology: An overview. In N. K. Denzin and Y. S. Lincoln (Eds.), *Handbook of qualitative research* (pp. 273–285). Thousand Oaks, CA: Sage.

———. (1990). *Basics of qualitative research.* Newbury Park, CA: Sage.

———. (1998). *Basics of qualitative research.* 2nd edition. Thousand Oaks, CA: Sage.

Stay, B. (1983). When re-writing succeeds: An analysis of student revisions. *Writing Center Journal, 4*(1), 15–28.

Storch, N. (2002). Patterns of interaction in ESL pair work. *Language Learning, 52*, 119–158.

Suri, H. (1999, July). The process of synthesizing qualitative research: A case study. Paper presented at the Annual Conference of the Association for Qualitative Research, Melbourne. Retrieved from http://www.latrobe.edu.au/aqr/ offer/papers/HSuri.htm

Bibliography

Thompson, I. et al. (2009). Examining our lore: A survey of students' and tutors' satisfaction with writing center conferences. *The Writing Center Journal, 29*(1), 78–105.

*Thonus, T. (1998). *What makes a writing tutorial successful: An analysis of linguistic variables and social context.* (Doctoral dissertation). Available from ProQuest Dissertations and Theses database. (UMI No. 9919428)

*———. (1999a). Dominance in academic writing tutorials: Gender, language proficiency and the offering of suggestions. *Discourse and Society, 10*(2), 225–248.

*———. (1999b). How to communicate politely and be a tutor, too: NS-NNS interaction and writing center practice. *Text, 19*, 253–279.

*———. (2001). Triangulation in the writing center: Tutor, tutee, and instructor perceptions of the tutor's role. *Writing Center Journal, 22*(1), 59–81.

*———. (2002). Tutor and student assessments of academic writing tutorials: What is "success"? *Assessing Writing, 8*(2), 110–134.

*———. (2003). Serving generation 1.5 learners in the university writing center. *TESOL Journal, 12*(1), 17–24.

*———. (2004). What are the differences? Tutor interactions with first- and second-language writers. *Journal of Second Language Writing, 13*, 227–242.

*Vallejo, J. F. (2004). ESL writing center conferencing: A study of one-on-one tutoring dynamics and the writing process. *Dissertation Abstracts International: Section A. Humanities and Social Sciences, 65*(02), 497.

Vygotsky, L. S. (1978). *Mind in society.* Cambridge, MA: Harvard University Press.

———. (1981). The genesis of higher mental functions. In J. V. Wertsch (Ed. & Trans.), *The concept of activity in Soviet psychology* (pp. 144–188). Armonk, NY: M. E. Sharpe.

*Waring, H. Z. (2005) Peer tutoring in a graduate writing centre: Identity, expertise, and advice resisting. *Applied Linguistics, 26*(2), 141–168.

Weigle, S. C., & Nelson, G. L. (2004). Novice tutors and their ESL tutees: Three case studies of tutor roles and perceptions of tutorial success. *Journal of Second Language Writing, 13*(3), 203-225.

*Welch, N. (1995). Migrant rationalities: Graduate students and the idea of authority in the writing center. *Writing Center Journal, 16*(1), 5–24.

*Williams, J. (2004). Tutoring and revision: Second language writers in the writing center. *Journal of Second Language Writing, 13*, 173–201.

*Wolcott, W. (1989). Talking it over: A qualitative study of writing center conferencing. *Writing Center Journal, 9*(2), 15–29.

*Woolbright, M. (1992). The politics of tutoring: Feminism within the patriarchy. *Writing Center Journal, 13*(1), 16–30.

*Young, V. (1992). Politeness phenomena in the university writing conference. *Dissertation Abstracts International: Section A. Humanities and Social Sciences, 53*(12), 4236.

* Entries with asterisks are those included in the synthesis.

INDEX

K

L

M

N

O

P

Q

R

S